INSTAGRAM

The Complete Guide for Effective Improving
Brand Awareness

(Secrets to Create a Brand and Become an
Influencer on Instagram)

Bernard Pritchard

Published by Andrew Zen

Bernard Pritchard

Instagram: The Complete Guide for Effective Improving Brand Awareness (Secrets to Create a Brand and Become an Influencer on Instagram)

ISBN 978-1-989965-82-5

Legal & Disclaimer

The information contained in this book is not designed to replace or take the place of any form of medicine or professional medical advice. The information in this book has been provided for educational and entertainment purposes only.

The information contained in this book has been compiled from sources deemed reliable, and it is accurate to the best of the Author's knowledge; however, the Author cannot guarantee its accuracy and validity and cannot be held liable for any errors or omissions. Changes are periodically made to this book. You must consult your doctor or get professional medical advice before using any of the

Table of Contents

Introduction

I'm about to let you in on a massive secret that not many business owners know out there... the number of followers you have does NOT matter. This isn't a book about how to grow your Instagram to 10,000 followers - it's about how to build a thriving business and generate leads and sales on Instagram. I started my social media marketing business in March of 2019. By October I handed in my resignation at my full time corporate gig because I was so overwhelmed with clients I'd had to start turning people away! I knew then it was time to take my side hustle full time. But guess what? I did all this with only 2000 followers on Instagram. Read that again. I didn't even have 10,000 - I wasn't even close to 5000! People expect that to have a thriving business you need millions of followers and they believe that's the only road to success. This is an idea that's forced into our heads daily. We see articles on the latest millennial billionaires with their huge thriving Instagram accounts. But the reality is there are thousands of business owners all over the world right now making an incredible life for themselves with only a small following on social media. In this book I'm going to break down that belief and throw it out the window. I want to show you how you can use Instagram to build a successful business with ease and have a dedicated following you know will always support you and keep coming back to buy more. It's not about how many followers you have, it's about how many customers you have. At the end of the day, it's just a vanity metric - a new follower doesn't pay the bills but a new customer does. Instagram recently made the decision to hide likes in several countries. This means followers cannot see how many likes an image has. Even the people at Instagram are now seeing likes do not hold the same value that they used to.I hope this book will help educate you on how to turn your followers into paying clients and live the life of your dreams. Let's get started!

Chapter 1: What Is Instagram And Why Should I Use It?

Before we get too far into marketing with Instagram, it is important to understand what Instagram is and why you would want to use it instead of another social media site in order to grow your business. Instagram is an app for social networking that was designed for sharing videos and photos from your smartphone. It does have some similarities to Twitter and Facebook in that when you create your own account on Instagram, you are going to have a profile as well as a news feed, but this one is really great for many businesses because it allows you to really showcase your business in a way that you just can't do with the other social media websites.

When you are on Instagram and you post a video or a photo, it is going to show up on your profile. The other people who are

4

following your account (we will discuss later how to get some more followers) will be able to see these new posts on their own feed. You will also be able to choose some followers to watch and when they post, you can see their information as well.

This is a pretty simple social media site to work with and some see it as a simplified version of Facebook, but it will focus mostly on visual sharing and using your phone rather than long posts and blogs. You will be able to use your account to interact with some of the other users who are on Instagram simply by following them, having them follow your account, private messaging, tagging, liking, and even commenting.

There are a lot of great devices running either Android or iOS that you can use in order to set up your free account with Instagram. In some cases, you can access the account from your own personal computer, but a lot of users like working with this social media site because they are able to use their smartphones in order to upload and share their media.

Before you are able to use this app, Instagram is going to ask you to create one of their free accounts. You can choose to sign up with your email account or with your Facebook account. You just need to come up with the username and password. While you are setting up the account, you may have a place where you will be asked if you want to follow some of the friends who are on your Facebook network on your Instagram one. You can choose if you want to do this now or skip it and do it later. (Or not at all!)

During this point, take some time to customize the profile by adding in a photo, a website link, a short bio, and your name. When you start looking for people who are going to follow you, or you decide to follow other people, they will want to know who you are so getting the profile set up will be a good idea.

As we mentioned above, you will want to use Instagram as a visual sharing site because this is the main purpose of using Instagram. You will want to find some of the best pictures and videos for your business and post these on your profile. You will also notice that every profile will also have a count that helps you to see who you are following and who is following you so that you can keep track of these numbers and make changes if you need. If you have someone who wants to follow you, they just need to tap on the Follow button and they can see what is on there. If you are a business, don't put the account to private or you will have to individually approve the request for all of them first.

An important part of working on Instagram, in addition to posting different media that works with your business, is to do interaction on posts and this can be really easy and a lot of fun. You can go on any post that you find and like and add a comment to it at the bottom, just make sure that your comments are well thought out and include more than just a few words. You can even use the arrow button in order to share it with someone else with the help of direct messaging.

The major thing that you will be doing with Instagram is sharing pictures, as well as some videos, that showcase your services or your products. What you post is going to vary based on what kind of business you are running, but you should make sure that the posts have value to your customers and that they really work with your business. Posting things from your recent vacation or from the meal that you had should be saved for your personal page, your business page is for your products and services and the posts should relate to this.

This can be a bit hard to think of when you get started, especially if you are just offering one service or just a few products that don't add in a lot of variety. Take a look through some other business pages that are similar to yours or in the same industry, and see what they used and what worked for them. This can at least get you started on some ideas and going in the right direction. You will want to change some of these around so that they are unique for your business, but it will really help you to get a good start.

If you are interested in finding some friends or even other interesting accounts to work with, you just need to use the search tab. It may not seem important to find other people on Instagram when you are a business, but finding these people to follow and commenting on their items and interacting with them can help other potential followers find you as long as you do all this work properly.

If you are looking to grow your business in a format that allows your customers to really get a good look at your products and services and that can be very interactive, then Instagram can be one of the best platforms that you will be able to utilize to really help you meet your own goals.

The Benefits of Marketing with Instagram

So why would you want to use Instagram for your marketing needs? Is it really that much better than some of the other social media sites, or are you just going to get on and find out that you are wasting your time or having to spend a lot more to get the results that you want? The good news is that there are many benefits to using Instagram for your business including the following:

Connect with your customers

When you think about connecting with your customers, you probably think about Facebook or maybe even Twitter to help you with that. But actually, Instagram is one of the most active when it comes to the user base and it is more likely that your followers will engage with you, interact, and even make purchases on Instagram compared to some of the other social media sites. In fact, a report that was done by Forrester Research found that your engagement can go up 120 times per follower compared to Twitter.

Businesses want to get communication and connections with your customers. They don't want to waste time doing all the work to just get a few people to respond to them. But with the high engagement that comes with Instagram, it is the best platform that you can use in order to connect with your customers, build relationships, and even listen to the feedback that you are given. While the other social media sites can work as well, they don't bring out the amount of engagement and potential sales as you can find with Instagram.

Learn what others like

If you have a business account set up already, your audience and followers could already be sharing the photos that you post and they could already be talking about your business on Instagram. This seems to be even more true for the brick and mortar businesses that have customers coming to their store on a regular basis.

For example, restaurants do well on places like Instagram because people like to share pictures of a new or favorite dish. Instagram makes it easy for them to do this because they can share that photo that they liked as well as allowing the customers to let others know where that meal is from. Restaurants are just one example of how this can work. You just need to post things that others will want to share and make sure that they are tagging your location as well. If you do this the right way, you will be able to get others to do some of the marketing for you.

If you would like to see if others have shared any of your photos and tagged your location is to do this as well. After you share the photo, you should be able to see a link that comes right above the photo and you will be able to click that link. This link is going to help you to see all of the photos that are shared from the office or the store and gives you a good idea of what some others are looking at in your business.

This is a good way to see which of your items are popular so you can make changes and pick out a new marketing plan. For example, if you have an item that is not doing the best, it may be a good idea to just skip on making that and focus on the items that do a little bit better so that you can get more shares and likes, and therefore more followers and sales, in the long run.

Reach a new audience

Instagram is set up to make it easier for the users to be able to discover new businesses, new people, and even new photos. This helps you out as a new business, but you need to make sure that you are taking the right steps to get other followers to find you.

One method that you can use to make people find you better is to use hashtags. This is similar to what you are able to do with some of the other social media sites. When you create a hashtag, you are adding a link to your pictures and videos. You can click on this link and view all of the other media that has been shared through Instagram with that hashtag. This allows you to become more readily available to the potential customers; when they place this hashtag into a search or some options that are similar, they will be able to see some of your media.

You as the business owner are able to use the hashtag as well in order to find some of your potential customers. You can search around for some of the keywords that you want and then meet some people who are sharing photos in your interest before making the introduction.

In addition to using these hashtags, Instagram has a cool think that is the Discover tab. This tab is dedicated to helping the various users to find photos that they want as well as helping them to connect with other users, or even other businesses, that are relevant to their needs.

Work with the other marketing channels

One thing that you will notice is that when you create some content on Instagram, even if you used some of their filters or other stuff to make the picture look better, you will be able to access and share it through all the different channels that you have for your marketing plan.

Within the settings inside of Instagram, you will be able to enable it to share your content on Twitter and Facebook. This means that if you upload some new photos to Instagram, they are automatically going to upload to your Twitter and Facebook accounts as well. you can even wait to share to the different networks until later, so that you use different release times, by saving the picture to the Camera Roll so that you can access them again later when you want to post.

In addition to using this content on your other social media accounts, you can also use it on your email marketing campaigns. Your settings inside of Instagram can be changed so that you can send some of your pictures and videos can be shown through email and other options to help make your marketing all work together.

Instagram and Facebook are created by the same company so you will find that these two in particular are able to work really well together. And since these two have the highest engagement and sales conversion out of all the social media platforms, it makes sense to combine them together to get even more sales for your business.

Generating sales

The main reason that you are on Instagram and other social media platforms is to generate more sales for your business. If you are able to create professional-looking images, you are going to have a better chance at promoting your product or even highlighting your services. and since you are able to use many of these social media sites for free (you can pay for a professional but often they are just going to do the same things that we talk about in this guidebook), this is a really affordable option to use.

Because all of this comes together, visual platforms, including Instagram are really successful at not only generating engagement, they are also able to drive up sales. And Instagram is able to bring in the sales more than some of the other options. One report from Shopify found that from Instagram, the average price for a sale on that site was $65. On the other hand, this average price is just $55 for Facebook and $46 for Twitter. This means that for the amount of work that you are doing, you could end up with much higher sales if you decide to use Instagram for at least part of the marketing campaign.

Of course, you need to make sure that you pick out the right media to post. You shouldn't fill up the feed with photos that have the same caption that just says "shop online" or "buy now" or something like that. Most people know that if you are a business posting a picture, you are trying to sell that item so find a way to be more creative and get their attention. Find cool and creative ways that you can display the products and then let the images do the speaking for you rather than using so many repetitive and boring sales tactics all the time. Telling a short story, using the right hashtags, and providing a quick link to your website in case the user is interested will be enough to get your sales.

Working with Instagram is not the only thing that is able to help you to see your sales go up, but when it comes to social media sites, this one is going to provide the highest response and conversion rates compared to other options like Twitter and Facebook. It is fine to use these as well, but if you want to start a marketing campaign with social media, it is definitely worth your time to add in Instagram to the mix.

There are many reasons that you should choose to go with Instagram to help you grow your business. It has higher engagement with the customers, which does translate into more sales, and will help you to get the results that you want. While it shouldn't be the only place that you do your marketing, it is a good place to get started to help your business soar.

Chapter 2: Basic Features

The characteristics of Instagram as a social platform whose contents are in relation to visuals. Its premises on sharing and viewing graphics, videos, and photos. Its operations and plugins are categorized on its contents: visuals. The idea that it is used only by young people is very wrong. In this section, you will be guided systematically into the features of Instagram for either beginners or professionals. By beginners, it means people that are new to Instagram while professionals mean those familiar or even have an account on the platform. Some of the basic features with their operations include:

The filter options

While uploading pictures on Instagram, the filter is the section which enables you to add enhancements on the photos to be uploaded. These filters make the pictures to look like studio edited ones. They are galvanized with features such as vintage, contrast, light, grayscale, soft glow, and lots more. Try uploading pictures and use this filter to create a special effect on them. Many influencers of Instagram claim that using these filters can make you outstanding among users of Instagram because the sense of filtration is typical only to you. Try it and grow your profile.

Like Button

One of the commonest features on Instagram is the like button. This platform can barely operate without features such as this. This is like an authorization given to fellow users to comment, follow or do anything to your post on the platform. The like button enables users to give either pleasing or unpleasing undertone remark on your posts. With the like button, lots of transformation like increment in the number of followers and the benefits that follow is activated. The like button works in two places: it can be used on the home page, and it can be used as a user's dashboard. When the like button is used at the general page, it only gives remarks on the posts while when it is on the user's dashboard, the person becomes a 'follower.'

The Iconosquare feature

This is a form of a hashtag that is typically used to track campaigns. The performance report of the campaigns is what Iconosquare brings to you. You will be able to see relating data of the hashtag and even the growth alongside engagement of it on the campaign you have created.

The @ feature on Instagram

This is used basically for direct comment. This is for comment on posts on the platform. One could comment by tapping on the comment bubble through the person's username or type @ alongside the username.

The Word Suggestion content

This feature has been designed to help while typing on the platform. With a few words, you will be given any suggestion to make it easier for you to type. In the cases of comment, you will see related words while searching for a username. You will have related usernames.

Instagram set up operations

To download the Instagram app, one needs to consider the iOS of the medium to download it. If you have Android, you will download from 'Google Play.' If you have an iPhone, you will download from the 'App store.' Search these stores, you will, with ease, locate the app.

Registering your Instagram Account

After downloading the Instagram app, you will need to open an account. The app should create a 'shortcut icon' on your homepage after installation: if it didn't check your installed apps. Register your account or log in if you have an account already.

Creating your Instagram Account

Upon the location and clicking on the app, you will need to create a username and password. Your username can be any name combination. At this point your creativity is needed, the username can be a nickname. Care must be taken to use a name familiar to the people in order to facilitate the location and gaining of followers quickly. For example, you might consider using a clip of your first name and surname in uppercase or lowercase as 'TIMSAM' or 'timsam' for Timothy Samuel. After the username, use a password that is familiar with other platforms. You will surely need to add your email account which you could create one for the account. You can choose to add your phone number or not.

Uploading your profile photo

After you have created your account, as part of the process of perfect and strong Instagram account, you will need to add your profile picture. The picture can be taken immediately as you open your account but uploading an existing picture with high quality is highly recommended. Select 'Done' when you have uploaded the picture.

Friends and Family found on Instagram

For capitalization of your account to the full fledge, you will need to follow people that will share your pictures, and you do same to theirs. You can consider giving them your username or search from your account. With increment in followers, there are lots of benefits attached to it.

Adding and Following on Instagram

To be added to an account, you will be on the followers' list. You can follow and be followed respectively. Addition of a user will as well enable you to follow too. However, to randomly add people, you could click on the 'cog icon' on the home screen and click on 'invite friends.' With this, contacts of people around your vicinity will be suggested.

Connect to Social Media

You have an option on the app to search your phonebook directly. Simply click on 'My Contact,' and you will be prompted to search. Contacts with the Instagram account will come up, click on 'Follow' to add them to your account. Then, click on the home icon to return to the home of your account which should show the added accounts.

Home Screen

The icon looks like a house. It will automatically refresh itself when your photo has like, comment or when one of your friends add photos. The home will be updated with data, however.

Profile

The brief story created about you is your profile. The file card at the corner of the home screen contains your profile. Other things at this corner are photos, "following" and "Followers."

Privacy on Instagram

On the 'Edit my Profile' button, you can restrict the people that can view your profile. This is not encouraging, however, for a business person.

Privacy Off/on

When your privacy is turned off, anybody, even outside Instagram, can view your account. When it is switched on, only people following you can view your account.

News Feed

Photos, graphics, and videos are what is contained in the news feed. You can refresh the page by simply swiping it down. The news feeds are selected randomly; you scroll up or down.

Viewing comments from your Friends and family

The photo at the top left of your home screen is used to view people that have commented on your photo. Before clicking on it, there is something in grey color. It is meant to give you information about the comment.

Adding comment

Simply tap the speech bubble at the home screen which will prompt a new page to enable you to write your comment. Send it, and your name will appear right under the comment.

Attached Links

This feature enables people to be prompted to either another user's account or website. It is strategically attached to the account to enhance it. Most likely, it is a business account. If you click on surf new page, you can return to your home by tapping the back button on your phone.

The # Hashtag meaning

This feature is used to publicize a given post. By publicizing it, very many users will have access to the post. When you are using the hashtag, make sure there is no space between it and your post to avoid misunderstanding of your post.

Additionally, when a hashtag is added to a post, it appears in blue. There are various reasons Instagram users use the hashtag. Some of these reasons include; promotion of business, gaining more followers, connecting to people that have the same idea and specialization as theirs, etc.

The hashtag enables you to search based on your specific interest on the platform. Your interest varies alongside many other things such as a book, mountain, etc. For instance, you could search with this #mountains. This will give you varying posts relating to your interest. Also, you will see profiles that have the same interest as you. The profiles that will be prompted will be top leading users who will teach you how best to construct your account too.

iOS, Android or Window icon

This particular icon is used to add photos. You can access it by clicking on the blue icon and then the circle at the bottom of the icon. Your gallery will be accessed automatically, and you can add your photo.

Followers icon

This is used to show the people that are following you in numbers. By followers, it simply means those people that your posts, whatsoever, will appear in their news feed. When you click on this icon, you will be able to see pictures of these people and either white color (to show you are following them) or blue button (to show you are yet to follow them).

Star symbols

This is technically referred to as the explore icon. It enables you to access a new page with a square at its top to type your information. With this icon, you can individualize your search. By individualizing, it means that you can search an account by hashtag or nickname. This facilitates a random and quick response from these people when you post. You can as well access their profiles upon searching.

Chapter 3: How To Create Powerful Posts

In this chapter, you'll learn the importance of having a systematic way of creating content.

I am not gonna teach you how to edit images, you can practice that in your own time and leisure.

But I will recommend some tools for editing that you can use for free or for as cheap as possible.

Here are the best editing tools to use for Instagram.

You have to have some kind of mobile device or tablet/iPad to use these applications.

A – Instagram

B – Fotor

C – Qwik

D – VSCO Cam

E – Lensical

F – PicLab HD

G – Photoristic HD

H – Handy Photo

I – Path On

J – Camera +

K – Photoshop Express

You don't have to have all of them.

In fact, just find one (or two) that you're comfortable with and just use it.

HOW TO CREATE A POST

Every image post will have 3 important parts.

The Image

For the image, you have to be clear of what you're trying to achieve.

Are you trying to motivate them? Are you trying to show them your product? Are you giving them a discount? Are you trying to engage them in a conversation?

Before you post an image, always be clear of your intentions.

Trying to shoe social proof + products?

Don't just post anything you can think of.

Try to be strategic in your posts and always have a goal for that one post.

Note:

Another thing you have to be weary of is consistency.

Don't use a lot of different filters or style in your photos.

If you use black and white, then don't make it a random post. Use it every 6 posts. Make it consistent.

Too many filters will make your Instagram look awful.

This one is actually pretty great:

This one, not so much. It feels random.

The Description

For the description, it should match your goal and your image.

If you have a post showing your bakery's cinnamon, then post something related to that image.

For example:

They say that cinnamon is good for the heart. We have no clue if it's true but Valentine's day is coming and couples are already flocking the store looking for our awesome couple deals!

Make it fun and make it sound original.

You can't be boring and expect people to generate conversation with you.

In some way, you have to be a little bit controversial sometimes.

Here's an example of what you shouldn't do or even if you do this, make sure that you don't do it a lot!

"Come to our store and buy our new couple's cinnamon rolls!"

It's just blatant sales pitch and that's not too fun for most people.

Here are some awesome descriptions:

A coffee shop aiming to get young customers. If you're target market is old people, then this description probably won't work.

Another example of a simple but awesome post.

The Hashtag

The next part of having a powerful post is the hashtag.

The hashtag is basically a way to:

A – Make other people discover you

B – To show what your photo is all about

With this in mind, every post that you have should ALWAYS satisfy these two guidelines.

When you're thinking of hashtags to use, try looking for other businesses related to yours and just copy what they're doing.

Are you selling Texas BBQ?

Then search for Texas BBQ and then see what others are using.

I recommend that you have at least 7-10 hashtags per post. Every hashtag is an opportunity to reach more people but too much may be too annoying for the eyes.

So search for your main term and...

Look for other hashtags related to your main hashtag.

As long as it is highly related to your post, you can also use these terms and get more customers!

Open some posts made by other pages and look at what hashtags they are using.

Then steal it! It's not like its illegal or something.

86 likes   1d

lamesato Last night at the
@smokesignalsbarbecue fam jam. Congrats
guys! The place looks amazing and the
BBQ is off the hook. These guys are gonna
kill it. #dundaswest #texasbbq
#bestieverhad

uncultured_mag Lovely post

Now that you know the anatomy of a powerful post, it's time to increase your followers!

Chapter 4: The Foundations Of Creating A Solid Long-Term Instagram Marketing Ecosystem

Powerful marketing campaigns can do wonders to transform the performance of your business. From struggling to make a sale to going viral in a day, anything is possible when your marketing campaigns are powerful enough to leave an impression on your customers. Optimizing your marketing campaigns for Instagram should be the core focus of every campaign you intend to run, and there's a lot of work that goes into creating just one campaign alone.

Time, effort, commitment, and not to mention, the budget that is spent, crafting a campaign to perfection until its ready to launch means you need to make sure all your bases are covered. This isn't as easy as it sounds, though, especially when your ideas and ambitions don't line up with the marketing budget you have to work with. Even with a limited budget, though, it's still possible to create powerful campaigns. A great campaign doesn't necessarily have to be accompanied by a big-budget all the time. It is still possible to do when you know how to work Instagram's advertising tools to your advantage.

7 Essential Steps to Create Powerful Advertising Campaigns

Creating powerful ad campaigns without having to break the bank requires careful planning and strategy. Plan your most powerful campaign using the guidelines below as a reference:

Step 1: Start with Your Best Objective

Your objectives list would probably have a few items on it, and it can be hard to narrow it down to just one. Every objective feels like it matters (and it does), but a powerful campaign requires focus. To do that, you need to pick the BEST objective out of that list and focus on that. Otherwise, you're going to end up with an ad that is trying to do too much at once, and at the end of the day, it ends up not being very effective at all.

It is always trial and error though when you're attempting to set up new ads, especially in the beginning, so don't get too frustrated and allow yourself some time to adjust to the process and get the feel of how things work best.

Step 2: Every Campaign Has a Name

Every campaign you plan should have its own name. Naming your ad is like a tracking system that is going to keep you organized, and it helps you keep track of what works and what did not. You can pick your campaign names based on campaign type, country, network, demographics, language, and basically anything that you'd like. That way, when you need to refer to a successful past campaign while planning your future ones, recollection is a lot easier and more detailed when you can quickly refer to Campaign A instead of trying to randomly recall bits and pieces.

Step 3: Deciding on Your Ad Placements

Instagram's Ad Manager feature provides you with a few ad placements options to choose from. You want to familiarize yourself with their options before you start selecting your target audience because it is going to help you decide if this ad is going to actually work well on Instagram, or if it would be best on another social media platform altogether. Ad placements must be edited according to the social media platform because it allows you to better track the performance of the ad. Your Instagram ad campaign should be optimized for the ad specific to the platform, avoid using a standardized format across all your social media profiles. A placement that works well on Instagram might not perform as well on Facebook or Twitter, for example, and vice versa.

Step 4: Zone In on Your Audience

Save yourself a lot of time and money by targeting the right audience group from the very beginning. Your target audience is going to be the tipping point of your campaign, the one that determines if it is a success or failure. To fine-tune your audience, reach, select them based on age, gender, location, language, demographics, behavior, and connections to name just a few. By zooming in on the details and fine-tuning your reach, you'll save yourself from spending precious dollars out of your already limited budget targeting the wrong group of customers who aren't going to yield any tangible results. Once you have selected the right audience group for your ad, you'll see the option of "Audience Definition" on your ads manager display. Use this function, because it is going to tell you if you have targeted your audience too broadly or too specifically.

Step 5: Customize Your Budget

The great thing about Instagram is the flexibility it offers when you need it. Like when it comes to budgeting, for example, which is completely customizable based on your needs. Since Instagram's advertising runs on the same platform as Facebook ads manager, what happens with the daily budget is that Facebook will spend a fixed or designated amount to help you deliver your ads each day on the campaign dates that you selected. The lifetime budget option lets you choose the amount you would be willing to spend during the dates of your ad campaign. Once you've chosen your budget, you will then select the schedule for which your ad will run. This will depend on the timeframe which you have set when you were planning the campaign in the initial stages. It is recommended that you choose the option on Instagram that states run my ad continuously starting today if you are looking to build brand awareness.

Step 6: Ad Format Selection

Once you're done setting your budget, schedule and deciding on who your target audience is, the next step of the process is to choose the Instagram ad format that you are going to go with. If you're on a tight budget, you're going to want to take your time carefully selecting the best ad format, so you get the most out of it. Different ad formats will produce different results, and with Instagram, the six different types of ad formats that you get to choose from are Carousel Ads, Single Image Ads, Single Video Ads, Slideshow, Instagram Stories Single Video, and Instagram Stories Single Image.

Step 7: Launch Campaigns with A Cause

Customers want to see that a brand is more than just focused on making sales and profits. They want to see that your brand cares about something other than its sales figures. A campaign that showcases your brand caring for a cause is a good way to shine the spotlight on your business. Your campaign for a cause should be a cause that your audiences will be able to relate to, something that resonates with them. For example, Dove launched its #DoveWithoutCruelty campaign, which emphasized the brand's commitment to not test its products on animals. Dove partnered with PETA and other social media influencers to promote this cause and it resonated well with a lot of other Instagrammers out there.

6 Practical Strategies to Maximize Your Marketing Campaign Potential

Instagram has made it easier than ever for businesses to sell their products and services on social media. Social media marketing today is not an option anymore. It's a necessity. Conventional advertising methods are slowly on their way out. If you want your business to get noticed, you need to be on social media. It's safe to say that every second you're not on social media is another second which is wasted because you could have been improving your brand awareness and driving sales.

Consumers these days prefer online shopping more than any other shopping method. The convenience that comes with online shopping is a huge incentive, and when these consumers are easily able to reach out and contact the brand, that motivates them even more because of the customer service experience that they receive. Powerful marketing campaigns help nudge your consumers in the direction to take action. While there may not be any sure-fire guarantees, what you can guarantee is that if you do the best that you can to ensure you're maximizing your campaign's potential, you stand a good chance of coming out on top.

Strategy #1: Be Short, Move Fast.

Social media is a fast-moving platform, and Instagram is no different. Customers spend only seconds on an image or video before losing interest and moving onto the next. They come here for the visuals and the videos, and they don't want to do a lot of reading. Keep your content to a maximum of 40 characters and nothing more, Instagram is the ideal example of a platform where less is more, in this case, especially when it comes to texts and words.

Strategy #2: The Power Lies in Your Visuals.

Not just images, but high-quality video content, too. Fantastic photos are what Instagram is all about. If you want to bring in the sales, boost your brand's reputation, and grab the attention of new customers, high-quality images need to be your no-break rule for every piece of content you produce with each marketing campaign. Customers these days are not about the hard sell anymore; they want something that is genuine and authentic to look at.

Strategy #3: Don't Overshadow Your Product.

A good rule of thumb to follow is that your branding should not be overshadowing your product. If it is, then you probably need to scale back on the branding a little bit. While you do need to feature your brand and logo on every content your produce, you may need to do it in a subtle manner so it doesn't appear like a "direct sales pitch" or hard sell.

Strategy #4: Working Landing Pages.

Customers will be extremely put off when they arrive at your landing page only to run into technical issues. All that hard work you put into your campaign is going to be futile if your landing page falls short since the customer won't be able to complete the final purchase anyway. Always test to make sure your landing pages are in working order so no one is left disappointed at the end of the day.

Strategy #5: Testing 1, 2, 3…

Run a couple of "test ads" on your Instagram stories and profile to see how your audience responds to it. Do they like your content enough to engage with it? Or is it not getting the response that you hope for at all? If it is the latter, it might be worth reconsidering if you'll want to spend money on this campaign. Test runs are a good indicator of whether your full-fledged campaign is going to work the way that you intend it to, which could end up saving you wasted money.

Strategy #6: Never Forget Your Call-to-Action.

The whole reason you're running this advertising campaign in the first place is because you want to see some real sales results. Without proper call-to-action, your customers are not going to know what needs to be done next. A call-to-action prompts and reminds them what the "next step" should be. Shop now, sign up now, apply now, contact us now, watch now, and download now are some examples of a call-to-action you should be using, depending on the nature of your campaign.

The 5 Best and Unknown Instagram Marketing Tips

We've become so used to seeing ads on our newsfeed these days that it feels like they have been around forever. Each day, as you scroll through any of your social media platforms (not just Instagram alone), within a minute or two, you're bound to encounter an ad. Maybe even within seconds of scrolling through your newsfeed, that's how common they have become. They may have been around for some time now, but businesses are still figuring it out, experimenting to see what works best, trying different tools and tactics as they get a feel for the feature, and determining what's going to work best for their business. There's always something new to be learned and discovered, as these social media platforms themselves continuously work to improve.

One of the reasons why navigating social media platforms is an ongoing learning process is because not every platform works in the same way. They each come with their own set of strengths, advantages, all of which can be used to help benefit a business's overall campaign goals. Instagram is no different. Being a platform, which is all about the visuals, Instagram is unique because it offers advertisers an outlet for them to get inspired. To discover new, creative possibilities and to bring those discoveries to their brand as they continue working diligently to enhance the experience of their audience and customers. Being an image-focused (and now video too) platform, first and foremost, Instagram hasn't lost its touch and stays true to that concept even though their ad offerings. They know it's because this is what the viewers have come to expect, what they have become accustomed to.

To get the most out of your marketing efforts on this platform, you need to position yourself one step ahead of your customers. Anticipate their needs, figure out what they want even before they do. Managing a social media marketing campaign is hard work, but there are certain tips and tricks you could take your profile, marketing, and advertising efforts from good to better, and finally, to exceptional.

Tip #1 – All Your Liked Photos in One Place.

Did you know that there's a quick way to view all the posts you've liked on Instagram in one place? Go to the "Options" tab, and then click on the "Posts You've Liked" selection. If you want to unlike any of them, just tap on the image and unlike the content. Don't worry, the user won't be notified that you've stopped liking their content.

Tip #2 – Saving What You Love.

View all your most-loved content and save them for easy viewing later on by simply bookmarking them. On your profile, you will notice that there is a bookmark icon at the top-right above your images. Tap on it, and select the "Collections" tab. If you haven't created one yet, simply select the "Create Collection" and start saving all your favorite content.

Tip #3 – The H.D.D (Hide, Disable, Delete)

Good business practice would be to not disable comments on your profile because this is one of your means of communication with your audience and customer base. However, if you do have to hide it, delete it, or even disable commenting for any reason, here's what you would need to do. Head on over to your "Options" tab once more, and then select on "Comments". Once you've done that, you'll have the option of filtering through your comments based on the keywords. Try toggling "Hide Inappropriate Comments" and key in the specific keywords which you're after so you can keep an eye out for comments that may not be the best fit for your profile. To delete comments, you'll need to head over to the speech bubble icon, which is located below the comment that you're looking to delete. You will then need to swipe to the left. There'll be a "trash can" icon that appears after you do this, and by tapping on that, your comment will be gone. If you're wondering whether you can disable comments entirely across your profile, the answer is no. Unfortunately, disabling needs to be done for each individual post. If you've got a post you don't want people commenting on, use the "Advanced Settings" option before you post your content. Choose the "Turn Off Commenting" option and no one will be able to post any comments on that particular post.

Tip #4 – That Extra Special Font.

There are always ways to make your profile stand out, one of which is by using special fonts. Ordinary keyboard typing limits your creativity because there's only one option to go with - whatever the keyboard presents you with. As always, third-party solution providers come to the rescue, and all you need to do is head over to these websites and copy special fonts from there. These fonts are not often found with Instagram and its community, so when you utilize these fonts, your profile will really stand out and be memorable. Websites like Instagram Fonts and LingoJam are a good place to start.

Tip #5 – Stay "Fresh" Without Deleting.

Delete all your old, outdated content without actually removing any of them from your profile. This keeps your profile looking fresh, updated, and always on-trend, the way your customers expect it to. Head to the post which you want to "remove" and then tap on the three dots at the top of the post. Next, select the "Archive" option to archive the content. You can review your archived content anytime by selecting the "Archive" icon, which is located at the top right corner of your profile page.

Chapter 5: Why Instagram Is Important For Employers

You may have some questions at this point. Why go through all this effort to post a few times on social media? Is it actually going to help my business, or am I just wasting my time? You have to keep in mind that, while social media has a lot of people floating around and a lot of big-time users, it takes time to build a following. Gaining followers isn't an overnight process, but if you continue to promote your profile, it will make your business more profitable.

Over 90% of marketers believe that social media marketing efforts increased their online visibility and communication between their business and social media users. It takes more time than traditional marketing does, but it is less stressful and can increase profitability. Brand awareness is going to be your greatest advantage when it comes to social media marketing. We have already discussed some techniques you can use to increase brand awareness for your company, but these techniques can also save you money when it comes to advertisement. For the most part, Instagram is free. You might be using some paid applications for post schedulers or paying a social media specialist to personalize your posts, but mostly it's a quick and easy way to talk about your brand and business without spending a ton of money. However, your company has the option to pay for online advertisements on different social media feeds and it will create pop-ups on different users' feeds. This will help them get to your website, and hopefully they will be following your social media as well once they have interacted on your company homepage. Instagram's formatting creates great opportunities for ecommerce businesses that are looking to break into social media marketing. If they want to use photos, videos, or the Instagram story ability, they can in order to attract more customers to their page. The visual concepts allow for businesses to market by showing off their actual products and displaying them in a modern way online. It's also a great way to keep your customers engaged and satisfied with your business. It's easy to review any comments and complaints and handle them effectively. Being able to interact with your company's customers will keep them happy. People like to have a voice, and when they see that a company is responding to their concerns, it keeps their satisfaction up. When customers see your company posting on social media, especially when replying to their queries and posting original content, it helps them build a positive image of your company in their minds. Regularly interacting with your customers proves that you and your business care about them. Once you get a few satisfied customers who are vocal about their positive purchase experiences, you can let the advertising be done for you by genuine customers who appreciate your products or services.

The other half of social media is SEO and conversions. Sharing content on social media gives users more reason to click through your website. The more quality content you share on your social media account, the more influx of website traffic you should see. As people read the information you put out in your posts, they will be more likely to continue on and visit your website. SEO requirements have changed from what they used to be. It used to be enough to just post on your company blog and make sure that your website and online newsletters were up to date. However, the Internet is looking at a lot more now. The more presence that you have on social media the better. Posting online creates consistency and validates your company's online presence. It also allows customers to click directly through to your website. You should have your company website posted on your profile page. Having direct access to a website allows people to avoid having to run through a search engine and see other options that pop up. By allowing people direct access to your website from your social media, you open yourself up to the opportunity to have more conversions for your company.

The more comfortable your business becomes with using Instagram and other social media platforms, the more productive you will become. Online businesses are becoming more popular every day. The fact of the matter is, the less that people have to shop around, the better it is for them. Being able to give your customers what they are looking for up front and supplying them with the option to avoid looking into other businesses is a way to create an immediate conversion. You want your followers to promote your company name and buy products from your business alone. Search engines have allowed people to find a huge variety of companies by what they are searching for. Now, social media has developed the same capabilities. It's the perfect place to build your company's reputation and promote sales from your page.

Building Sales Through Social Media

The entire point of marketing is to bring in sales. At the end of the day, your goal is to make that conversion from a viewer to a buyer. The first thing you need to do to make sales is to be present on the same platform that your customers are on. If you are looking for a young adult to adult market, then Instagram is the place to be. LinkedIn is more business-based and can be useful if you're looking to sell to other businesses. If you want to avoid some hassle, find the right market before you begin advertising your products. There are websites like Keyhole that can help you determine the age market that you are looking for.

Next, you have your influencers. Influencers make selling things easier because their followers are tuned into their market. You can also give your influencers a promo code which helps you track the effectiveness of their advertisements, but also promotes your business and gives people a discount for buying your product at the same time. For example, a lot of makeup business will use beauty bloggers to promote their products and, in turn, give them a promo code to sell the product at a discount of around 10-15% off. As a result, people will return to the beauty blogger for discounts on products, and it allows customers to buy the products at a lower rate. You get the benefit of a sale while the blogger gets a follower.

Brand advocates are also a great way to help promote your business. Brand advocates are a little different than influencers because they might not be popular on social media. However, they know your product and they like using it. Brand advocates are the way to go if you don't want to use an influencer. Real people can be enticed to promote products for you through their social media by being offered free products or discounts on items. Offering free stuff is a great way to get into anyone's good graces, especially if those items are usually on the more expensive side. This is how jewelry companies and makeup companies make some good investments by utilizing bloggers and influencers. The cost of a product is usually cheaper than paying someone to promote your business. The best part about brand advocates is that they already like your business. You're giving them a product that they already like, and they have already posted that they like your brand. You can then use this relationship to your advantage. The best way to sell something is to not have to say a word. Think about it like this: if you are shopping for an engagement ring, you're going to visit multiple stores, and the associates are going to try to upsell you on warranties and other products. You might feel like you are being overwhelmed by information. Hearing positive reviews from other people, though, will help you feel more comfortable. You want a company to care about you and the product they are selling, so hearing from someone else that they trust this brand and the company's work will go a long way in the eyes of other customers.

Another great way to involve customers in the sale experience is to promote their content. A great example is Coca-Cola. When you tag them in a post on Instagram, they often reply to your comment or picture, which increases the product experience for that person. When a company shares someone else's post, even if it does feature their product, they are showing the proof that people like this product. You can also drive more sales through social media by encouraging your customers to share their photos online. Be sure to take the extra step and share these user-generated photos on your own social media profiles. This is an easy way to increase loyalty with your existing customers, and it adds credibility to your brand whenever potential customers visit your social media profiles (Barker, 2018). Creating a brand hashtag not only increases brand awareness; it also allows your followers and product users to share their brand experiences with others. When you see the posts and photos that you are tagged in, you have the opportunity to respond and comment on their photos, increasing your interaction rating in the algorithm.

Remember, you want your company page to be as popular as possible with more followers, likes, and comments in order for the algorithm to push you into the trend pages and promote your company's Instagram. So, even when you are simply sharing your followers' tagged posts, you are still increasing your overall rating in the algorithm due to your activeness on the platform.

Your Instagram posts should also teach your customers about your business. This comes back to the idea that your posts should encourage your customers and clients to follow your page to your company website. By providing how-to content in your posts, you will be providing customers with the information that will inspire them to try your product and see what all the rage is about. Other companies will be drawn to your page if you post tips and advice on how to improve on your business and how to market products. Not everything has to be business on the platform, and sending friendly well wishes to your customers around the holidays is pretty typical as well. However, in order for people to know what your company is doing and for you to promote your business products, your posts should consist of techniques or strategies that your company is using, or quick video clips of a specific product being used. Think about how car commercials work when you want to get an idea of how to draw people in. Sometimes, these commercials only show a small part of the car, like the wheels spinning or the headlights turning on, and it's just enough to get you to imagine the whole picture and the capabilities that this sleek new car could have. It makes you want to look into that product even more. The teasers of a good product are enough to turn people's heads.

The Future in Internet Marketing

If you're still not convinced that internet marketing and social media platforms are the way to go, then you need to think about the future. Online marketing has already become very dominant on the scene, but by the time the year 2020 comes around, more and more people will be using their mobile phones and handheld tablets to do the majority of their shopping. When physical printing becomes obsolete, the online market will be the only thing left.

Now is the time to be perfecting your skills in internet marketing, especially in the realm of social media. Over the next few years, Generation Z will be growing up, and they will become the major consumers of the era. Since this generation grew up surrounded by technology, they were raised with YouTube videos and smartphones instead of TV advertisements and magazines. They have entirely different priorities than the generations before them, but they also have a different way of looking at life. Due to the fact that they are raised with technology, they never have to wait for much and have instant access to whatever they need, including buying things online. Generation Z is referred to as having an 8-

second filter, which they use to find content that they care about and actually want to look at. They don't have to waste any time scrolling through loads of information when they can just bypass it by finding exactly what they want.

Companies are now having to figure out how to capture the attention of this generation and keep them focused on the product being sold within an 8 second time frame before they move on. If they can't capture their attention and hold it, the sale will be bypassed and they will move on to the next segment of their news feeds. However, it isn't just this generation that is turning to technology for shopping. More and more businesses are closing their physical doors due to online shoppers. Warehouses are limitless in terms of the internet, and people don't have to wait in line to get what they want. Shopping online has become as easy as clicking three buttons and tapping the screen to pay for something online. With the age of online shopping on the rise, marketers need to be prepared to keep up.

In order for companies to stay profitable in a constantly changing technological world, they need to be able to focus on the trending topics and platforms of that moment. Advertising on Facebook used to make major waves because that was the platform where most people were looking and making friends. You could follow company pages and that would be enough. However, now Instagram has become the most popular social media platform for people; it offers a wide variety of photo and filter options, story abilities, and other features that the other social media platforms don't have. By advertising and building marketing strategies for Instagram, there is the option to create a quick and easy link directly to the company website that's posting the ad. The posts also don't stand out as ads right away, but look similar to any other Instagram post until you notice the "swipe up" banner at the bottom that will take you to the shopping site.

The Internet is the future of all resources. Marketing is becoming entirely digital and is moving away from physical print due to the fact that fewer people are buying anything physically printed. With practically everyone online in the social media world, selling a product has never been easier. Instagram users are not only more engaged, but they are also usually online shoppers. A study recently showed that 72% of Instagram users made a purchase decision after seeing something advertised on Instagram. The most common categories that saw sales were clothing, makeup, shoes, and jewelry. Instagram shoppers are easy to convert when it comes to sales because they know what they are looking for in products. They are following the brands they like, and as they discover new trends in their newsfeed, they continue to buy new products that suit them. That's why Instagram is so high on the charts for influencer marketing. People are following beauty bloggers and trend setters that have unique styles because they want to be on the same path as they follow their brand ambassadors' advice on what to buy and what to wear.

Internet marketing has become more prominent in recent years due to the fact that people are buying more products online than they are from physical stores. Through social media, and Instagram in particular, it's becoming easier to go from advertisement to webpage with the swipe of a finger. There are different banners that can be displayed on advertisements, including ones that say "Learn More" or "Shop Now" at the bottom of the picture. These allow you to simply swipe the line upward, and it will automatically load the business website for you from the advertisement you were looking at.

Chapter 6: Strategies To Grow Your Following On Instagram.

The more followers you have, the higher the chances of you engaging with users and offering them unique experiences. However, growing the number of your followers is not an easy feat, and many brands try to take the easy route. They do this by paying for likes or followers on the tons of websites offering these services. But the truth is, if you want to get the best results for your brand, you will have to grow your audience organically.

What this means is that, regardless of the number of followers you currently have on your profile, if they are not genuine, they are not heading to your landing page or store. Also, it means they are not telling others about your website or the services you render, nor are they buying anything you sell. This is an important reason for you to pay attention to growing an organic and genuine audience on your Instagram page, or any other social media platform, for that matter.

Why Do You Need to Grow Your Followers Organically?

Here are some of the reasons you need to grow your followers the right way on Instagram:

Access to More Features

Features like Instagram stories are great for sharing the story of your brand. The story feature has been observed to amass a higher level of engagement in comparison to other formats. Besides, the stories feature can be a massive source of revenue and traffic. Using this feature, you can share a link to other websites on Instagram. The other site in this instance could be your store, and it is made possible using swipe-ups. This is the only other location you can share links aside from your bio which lets you share a link.

More Followers Translates to Enhanced Reach

Instagram is a platform that remains organic. Even though there are solutions that require payment, it is still possible for you to engage and reach a sizable number of your audience without the need to invest any cash whatsoever.

For this reason, the more people following your page, the more the possibility of them coming across your content and engaging with it. Also, using a well-planned-out hashtag strategy will ensure you get great results.

More Followers Means More Credibility

You may not like it, but the fact is that having lots of followers on Instagram translates to credibility. It is the same way influencers operate. If you are offering great content consistently, lots of people will engage your content, like and share it. In doing so, a higher number of individuals will do the same, and so on. The number of people following your account has a way of influencing any choice not to follow or follow you. This is the reason so many marketers are tempted to pay for follows - the credibility factor.

Strategies to grow your following

Ensure Your Account Is Optimized

The very first and easiest step in growing your Instagram followers is to optimize your account. Like we have covered earlier, this has to do with creating a great bio and profile. If there is no profile image, username, or bio, people will not know your brand owns a specific account. This may not seem important, but lots of brands fail to add a link on their bio to a landing page, while some even fail to fill it in the first place. This is your number one location for driving traffic from Instagram to your website, so it is vital to take all the steps in fully optimizing your account.

Post Content in A Consistent Manner

A great way of dealing with this is to ensure your posting schedule is consistent. Typically, brands should not post more than a few times each day. However, regardless of the route you choose to take, make sure it stays consistent. More than 200 million users on Instagram check out the website each day, so to spread your reach more, you can spread your posts all through the day. By adopting a schedule and sticking to it, you will be able to develop a consistent experience for your followers.

Create a Schedule for Your Posts Beforehand

There are many tools you can use to easily schedule content for your Instagram profile in advance. When you do this, every member of your team will be able to see schedules and campaigns more effectively. It is a wise decision to plan your content using scheduling tools, as they can let you reach your target audience and also maintain a consistent content flow. A few tools that can help with scheduling include Later and Hootsuite, among others.

Encourage Other Accounts to Post Your Content

An excellent method of making sure more users follow you is to be present and get your brand into the feeds of your clients. You need to do this on other Instagram pages in addition to your own. An easy way to get into the feeds of your customers is to sponsor UGC (user generated content). Also, you can run contests on Instagram to ensure your brand reaches a broader audience.

Learn How to Tell Real Followers from Fake Ones

Like we covered earlier, there is a difference between an account on Instagram with fake followers and one with authentic ones. It may seem less challenging to buy Instagram followers, however, the downsides outnumber the benefits.

Promote Your Instagram Page

One of the top ways of ensuring users discover you is to develop awareness and visibility. If your goal is to increase the number of followers on your Instagram page, it is important for you to let them know where they can find you. If you own a blog or website, you could incorporate social media buttons to any of them as this will help encourage users to share your content and let them know where to locate you on Instagram.

Post Content Your Audience Desires

Watch out for recent trends on Instagram so you can be sure you are posting content that is trending at that moment. To make this less complicated, you can capitalize on Instagram analytics tools as they will make it less difficult to analyze and track Instagram content.

If you are not sure about where to begin in regards to your content strategy, you can check out what your competitors are doing. However, it is not advisable to just copy what they do. Instead, take a look at the way they post, pick ideas, and improve upon those ideas. This can set you ahead of the game. With what you learn from your competitors on Instagram, you will quickly see what is providing results for brands in the same sector as you.

Get the Discussion Started

Starting discussions is a great way to announce your presence to users on Instagram. In a quarterly report released by social media analysis company Sprout Social, over 35 percent of customers used social media to contact customer service in the second quarter of 2016. This means that social media outranked email, live chat, and in-store customer care. This implies that the number one customer reference for businesses is social media. To boost your sales and the integrity of your brand, your company should be communicative and supportive on Instagram.

Ensure Your Users Participate

User-generated content is one method businesses are using to encourage users to partake. This form of audience promotion can spur people to share content across many accounts and cause you to trend using your branded hashtags. This sort of outreach is just about what your business needs in gaining more followers on Instagram.

Ensure You Make Your Followers Happy

A happy customer is a returning customer. This also implies to your Instagram followers. When you make it your goal to put a happy face on your followers, you increase your audience growth rate. These crucial tips will assist you in extending your social reach, increasing the visibility of your content, and building you a loyal audience.

Be Faithful to Your Content Strategy

Ideally, your target followers should get a good idea of what your brand is really all about within a few seconds of visiting your profile. Your posts should tell you what you really care for and what you could offer for your audience who are looking for the same images in their feeds in the future.

Join the Instagram Stories Bandwagon

Instagram Stories is one of the most effective tools for attracting a massive following. This will provide your followers a sneak peek into your brand, the people behind your team, and it also increases engagement to record heights. Instagrammers like to see raw and real posts, so be sure to post stories that are not too formal or salesy without compromising your content strategy.

Engagement Over Volume

The quality of your followers is a crucial element in Instagram marketing. A brand with 1,000 followers who are regularly engaging with your content is far more valuable compared to a brand with 100,000 random followers composed of people who are not all qualified to be your target audience. You should attract followers who can resonate with your posts, so they can share them and interact with your online community.

Use the Recommended Image Size for Instagram

Using the ideal size for your Instagram images will substantially improve the aesthetic appeal of your feed, which could translate to more followers. Take note that the standard image size for Instagram is 1080 px by 1080 px. This is different from the previous standard Instagram post of 612 px by 612 px.

Hold Instagram Promos

Holding Instagram-exclusive promos, contests, and events can significantly boost not only the number of your followers but also your engagement. Despite the many advances in the modern world, customers are still attracted to freebies and giveaways.

Just be sure that your promos will result in more followers or could improve engagement. In addition, your promo mechanics should be clear, and you should be specific on how you want your followers to participate in the promo.

Use Instagram Shoppable Posts

Now, what are Instagram Shoppable Posts? This is a recently-added feature that allows users to do their shopping straight from Instagram and without having to leave the app. Instagram shoppable posts are labeled with a shopping bag icon at the lower left corner (top right corner for business profiles) of the post, or with a pop-up that says, "Tap to View Products." This feature also allows users to browse through your "Shop" feed directly from your profile.

Always Have A Solid Call To Action

You may think that Instagram is purely a visual platform, but the presence of the caption box is one way you can turn browsers into shoppers. Potential customers prefer to be told what steps they should take when they're shopping online. Your CTA or a call to action, however need not be too complex. Just a simple message inviting users to go a little step further should do. It could be something like "Impressed? You can own one, too, by clicking the link in our bio." Just make sure all your links are working and that the one in your bio leads to the right page where the exact product is located.

Use Promo Codes

Promo codes are always a great way to make customers stick around. While it's a real challenge to get customers make their first purchase from your shop, placing a discount offer they can't resist will help convince them to buy from you. When you reward your customers with such, you are adding value not only to your service but to them, as well. This is an excellent way to retain customers, because when your followers know that they can regularly enjoy discounts from you, they are more likely to be loyal customers. With the right hashtag, this tactic will not only drive conversions but high share counts at the same time.

Initiate A Contest

Loyal Instagram users love a good contest every now and then. Even those who do not win enjoy the thrill of waiting whether they'll get the grand prize or not. The key to a successful contest is giving away one of the top items in your product line. No one wants to join a contest and win a cheap prize. If you can offer your customer the best that you have, they won't think twice browsing through your shop knowing how good your products are.

Take Advantage of User-Generated Content

It would be gold if customers would spontaneously post photos of themselves with your product on it and then tag you, but that doesn't happen all the time. One way you can encourage your followers instead is through a contest, like offering a huge discount to the first 100 customers to put your product on airs with a hashtag of your choice.

Reach Out To Customers and Followers Individually

Encourage your customers and followers by sending them personalized message. It could be about new products and promotions. You can even reach out to them just to reward them with some free merchandise or promo codes. Aside from personal messages, a comment on one of their Instagram posts would be greatly appreciated. People love it when you give them attention, and when you invest your time in them, they will return the favor with their loyalty and wholehearted support.

Automation

You have to understand that there are automation tools (which may also be referred to as 'bots') on Instagram that are spammy, and can impact the user experience of your followers in a negative way. These are tools that let you automatically follow other people's account and comment on their posts. That is simply unacceptable as it produces spam, which we all don't like.

Schedule and Optimize Posts For Maximum Engagement

Scheduling your posts is a huge part of automation. In fact, it's safe to say that it's the most important part of the entire process. When you're using Instagram for business, it's very different than when you're simply doing it for personal use. With your personal account, you can post whatever you want to post and whenever you feel like posting. It's spontaneous, and you care very little about what others might think. You just can't do that with your Instagram business account.

Curate High-Quality Content from Your Community

Content curation allows you to update your feed more regularly. It's also great way to establish your reputation as a thought leader, as well as offer your followers fresh points of view regarding your brand. Instead of having to come up with enough content to publish multiple times a day or a week, you can leverage your community by reposting their images. One way you can do this is by creating a branded hashtag and encouraging your followers to post about your brand using the hashtag. Once there's enough people using your branded hashtag, you can collect the best among the group and import them into your queue using whichever tool of your choice.

Learn to Use Filters

As stated by Canva (n.d.), the most utilized filter on Instagram is Clarendon. With this filter, you can highlight your images, brighten them, and also add shadows to make them appealing. Use a constant filter that tallies with the persona of your brand and offers it a consistent and distinct look. According to a study carried out by Yahoo Labs and Georgia Tech, utilizing filters and including amazing copies to pictures could help enhance viewability by as much as 21 percent. It can also lead to a 45 percent enhancement in the number of comments (Friedman, 2015).

Exploit Hashtags

To get the best from your content, you can try incorporating branded hashtags into each post. In doing so, you can link them to your brand, and oversee them with the aid of a tool for social media listening. There is no right amount when it comes to the number of hashtags you will be able to include in captions. However, it is vital to remain relevant and add hashtags that have to do with anything you post on Instagram. It is not ideal to fill your posts with irrelevant hashtags, all because you want more. Doing this can have a negative impact instead of the positive one you desire.

Repost Content from Brands Similar to Yours

What if you don't have the time to develop quality content for yourself? The great news is that it is not essential. If you are in a viable niche, there is a high possibility that there are other accounts consistently developing content that piques the interest of your audience.

Integrate Polls in Instagram Stories

Individuals and brands now can include engaging polls to their stories. In addition to being entertaining, these polls are a great means of engaging with your audience and getting their opinions on various subjects. By taking advantage of the change to get the opinion of your audience on a decision or subject, you could help save money, energy, and time which could be channeled to other areas of your business.

Tell an Actual Story of Your Brand

The introduction of stories has proven that there is significant value in authentic content in the eyes of your audience. For this reason, when you document your journey, your brand becomes more approachable. This means you need to use your stories to tell a real story. Tell stories concerning the services and products you provide. This can help in developing the loyalty of brands, which increases the possibility of referrals and purchase.

Make Quality Posts Frequently

Instagram, as we covered earlier, had the most levels of interaction in comparison to other social media platforms. Your followers are available to create connections with you. However, you have to provide something for them to engage with first.

Users are always in search of timeliness and stability from the businesses and brands they follow. Additionally, the Instagram algorithm puts your presence on Instagram into consideration when trying to determine where to place you on the Explore Page. But, when you begin to plan a consistent schedule for posting, you have to attain the right timing as we have covered earlier. It won't be of any benefit for your followers consisting of professionals if you make posts during the day when they would be at work.

Chapter 7: Turning Your Followers To Become Customers

Social media is without a doubt an essential component of a successful digital marketing strategy. It's one of the best mediums to boost your brand's awareness and reputation online — where first impressions are important.

More likes, shares, and followers are all great for your online reputation, but social media can provide your business with more valuable things than that. This is why small businesses are doing their best to make a name on social media as it's possible to convert follows into new customers.

However, it takes strategic planning and persistence to get more customers from your social media marketing. This chapter will talk about that.

4.1 Using Promo Codes

Who doesn't like a discount? Giving away promo codes to your followers is one of the best ways to turn your followers into clients. The benefits of doing it on your Instagram is that it doesn't require the follower an effort to get the promo code, it's easily available to them by just scrolling and remembering the codes written. You can also add a link that initiates a call to action to your followers – this link leads them to the website where the code is going to be automatically used.

Popular Ways of Sharing Discount Coupons on Instagram

There are several ways for you to share the discount codes successfully. Here are those ways:

If you would like to give away a promo code during a special holiday, then design your coupon with images related to this occasion. Add texts to the image, stating the value of the coupon along with instructions on how to redeem it. You can put the code in the photo, however, it is necessary that the discount is clearly shown in it. Also, don't forget to write thedate validity in the description as well as the terms of use.

If you want to take it to the next level, you can even create a video to distribute the promo code. The success of this campaign heavily depends on your creativity.

If the promo code you are giving away is only valid for 24 hours, then posting on your Story would be the perfect option. This way of giving away coupon code is the most popular way used by companies today.

Most active Instagram users upload and watch stories every so often – it really replaced Snapchat today. This has become a favorite feature of people who keep certain aesthetic on their Instagram account as they don't need to spend more time taking multiple pictures and edit them just to pick the best one to upload as the posts disappear after

24hours anyway (unless you put them in
the Highlights).

Chapter 8: Growing Your Followers

This can be a difficult stage because it involves getting more people to follow and keeping those already following you engaged, so they don't unfollow you. One of the easiest ways to get your followers entertained and engaged, and to gain more followers is by running contests.

Run a contest

The main reason why people go on social media is to get entertained and get a momentary break from real life.

Getting your followers involved in a contest is an excellent way to keep them entertained and still be able to pass your brand message across.

You don't have to spend all your money because you are running a contest, you can be on a budget and be able to run your contest successfully. The primary key to making your contest turn out right is by coming up with a good idea and having a solid implementation plan.

Strategies and steps to take to ensure that the contest you run turns out a success.

If you don't make time to plan out your contest or giveaway, you will end up spending money or giving out products for free without it adding a profitable return to your business.

The steps to take include:

1. You can partner with another brand which products complement yours. For example: If you have a shoe line, you can partner with another company that is into fashion. If you are selling skincare products, you can partner with a brand that sells beauty products. You just have to choose a brand that has a similar audience to yours. When picking a brand ensure you will gain at least 50% from the partnership. You can decide with the other brand the best account to host the contest.

2. Pick a prize that will attract your followers and get them excited. Whether you are picking cash or products as the prize, make sure it is attractive enough.

3. Another strategy you can use is using a popular Instagram influencer. When you partner with an influencer, tell them to host the contest on their page so their followers can pay a visit to your own page. Pick an influencer that has a similar target audience as yours.

4. Ensure you set up definite rules that will serve as a guide for your followers when entering the contest. An example of a rule to set is follow @youraccount, then tag X # of your friends.

5. A lot of people think they stand the chance of getting more followers or engagement on their page when they run contests or giveaways for weeks. When you run a contest for more than a week, people will get bored and lose interest in your contest. Run it as fast as you can, not more than 6 days. The ideal period of time

to run it is 3 days. Also, avoid running contests very often, otherwise people will only follow you only for your contests, and quickly unfollow you, instead of following you for what you offer and represent. Running a contest once every 2 months is a good start.

Keep them involved

Another way of keeping your community engaged is by giving them something to do.

If you want to keep someone busy or engaged, get them involved so they can feel as a part of your project. This can also help in building a relationship of trust between your brand and the followers.

Involving them could include asking them to like, if they agree with the post you uploaded, asking them to tag a friend or share the post, or even sharing their thoughts or ideas. It's just like a teacher giving her students an activity to do after lessons. This will help her know if she's going in the right direction and it will also increase interaction.

Whatever task you want to give your followers should be something they will enjoy doing. It shouldn't be done frequently or it will become tiresome.

Emojis

Using emojis is a smart method for creating a pattern interrupt in your post. Pattern interrupt is a call-to-action method for interrupting and changing what your audience is doing. It helps to highlight your post and stand out from others.

Post consistency

A lot of people have different opinions on how often you should post. Most think that you need to post so many times in a day. If you fall into that category, you are getting it wrong. The primary key here is consistency. Making one or two posts every day is good practice. However, you need to know that you need to maintain whatever speed and frequency you begin with, to ensure you are consistent. Create a pattern for how often you will post or when you will post. Don't you think your brand will start sticking to your followers' memories if they get a post notification from you at a particular time every day?

Time

There's no formula to this one. The best way to work out a perfect time to post is to find out the time zone of your target audience. Most times, people tend to check out their social media accounts in the early mornings so they can know what's going on and what the day has in stock for them. They login in the middle of the day while taking a break from work or in the evenings when they are back from the day's activities. Target these periods and ensure they align with the time zone you are targeting. Sometimes, you may not be able to meet up, don't beat yourself up. During days like that, you can just go ahead and post. Just don't go posting at midnight, most people will be asleep then. An Instagram post has a minimum of four hours before it becomes buried in followers' feeds, so when you post at midnight your post won't get the chance to be seen.

Follower Software

Many brands avoid addressing this, but trust me, most of them use this type of tool. I don't recommend using follower software, as it goes against the terms and conditions of Instagram, but it's important that you know how they work. Note that using a follower software might get your account blocked and even banned on Instagram, so avoid using it. I'm telling you this only for informational purposes.

Follower software allows you to find a large group of people that are interested in a particular thing.

Some follower softwares allow you to see the people that follow a specific brand. This is particularly useful for benchmarking purposes. They should be able to hide which users you have followed and unfollowed in the past, so you don't end up following the same set of people again, and allow you to unfollow those that haven't followed you back. One positive thing about these tools is that they make it easier for you to unfollow people that are not interested in what you do, and unfollow bots, which is good as bots only hurt your engagement and reach. Some follower softwares are Skim and Combin.

REMEMBER: Instagram restricts a maximum of 200 follows/unfollows daily and 10 follows/unfollows per hour; however, these numbers vary per Instagram user, so they can be more or even less for your account. As I mentioned before, if you exceed these limits, your account will be blocked from activity for 1, 2 even 4 days, or you might even be banned for life. Always remember to obey Instagram's terms and conditions, and engage with people from your niche to increase your engagement.

***DISCLAIMER: I am not recommending the use of these tools. This topic and ebook i s for general informational purposes only. All information on this ebook is provided in good faith, however I make no representation or warranty of any kind, express or implied, regarding the accuracy, adequacy, validity, reliability, availability or completeness of any information on this ebook. UNDER NO CIRCUMSTANCE SHALL I HAVE ANY LIABILITY TO YOU FOR ANY LOSS OR DAMAGE OF ANY KIND INCURRED AS A RESULT OF THE USE OF THE FOLLOWER SOFTWARE OR RELIANCE ON ANY INFORMATION PROVIDED ON THIS EBOOK. YOUR USE OF FOLLOWER SOFTWARE AND YOUR RELIANCE ON ANY INFORMATION ON THIS EBOOK IS SOLELY AT YOUR OWN RISK.

Like other people's posts

Everyone likes for their posts to be appreciated and will always return the favor when you do that for them.

Liking other people's posts is an awesome way to increase the engagement on your page. Keep in mind that the maximum number of likes is 1000 a day; however, this number is different for each account. Again, exceeding this number might get you banned from Instagram, so be very careful.

Use the Right Filters

Filtered pictures are likely to be viewed and commented more than unfiltered pictures.

Using the right filters will create a distinct difference in your engagement in a positive way. Filters change the results you get in your engagement drastically. Sadly, lots of brands don't know it makes a difference.

The best filters to use that will increase the chances of a dramatic change in the views and comments are those ones that create:

Warm temperature

Higher exposure

Higher contrast

These are the best filters to use when it comes to uploading on Instagram. Higher exposure filters tend to generate more views, while warm temperature filters tend to draw in more commenters. Using saturation or age effect filters tend to lead to lower views and comments respectively, so avoid using these ones.

Advertising

This is an option you can try out if you don't mind spending some money. The positive thing about advertising on Instagram is that it is not expensive at all and it is very cost-effective. You can advertise for Instagram with the awareness advertisement. While running the ad, you can link it to other ebooks or to your Instagram account if you want to increase your followers.

It will cost more to use this method to build and get more followers, but it is worth every penny. This is because you will be able to target your audience specifically.

Chapter 9: Trending

How do I stay in trend?

As mentioned in the previous chapter, you should understand your focus, your target audience, and the type of content you plan to post on your Instagram blog.

The content you share on Instagram will be shown via your photos and videos.

Generic images and videos that have no particular relevance to your blog or what it represents cannot be compromised on your content.

Your content should be:

Relatable—The audience needs to be able to connect with the content on your blog. Relatability is important.

People will not feel the need to follow something they cannot relate or connect with.

Relevant—Your content cannot be outdated. Your posts must be related to each other.

Randomly posting images or videos that don't correlate with your audience.

They will not be convinced by what you are claiming to offer.

Informative—Your audience must be able to receive something from your blog.

You must strike a balance between posting attractive images and/or videos and the information the audience needs. Information is often found in the headings of the images.

Eye-catching/Esthetically pleasing—Remember that Instagram is a visual platform.

It's all about the pictures.

You must ensure that your photos are of the highest quality and the most original.

Try not to copy the photos of other people—the last thing you need is legal problems about something that can easily be avoided.

Put in the work required to create original and creative posts for your audience to enjoy.

It's a good idea to remember your target audience before you create content for your page

—you can't expect to reach every single user on Instagram. It's not realistic or practical.

Too many users have different interests and preferences to try to use them all.

Find the audience who sees what you have to offer as helpful, enjoyable, and beneficial.

There are always people on the platform who are interested in your content, no matter what.

Why does my content need to be effective?

The main purpose of your content should be to evoke your followers' reactions.

They should feel obliged to see more of your content and more about what you have to offer.

Followers should share their content with their own supporters.

You should feel that your content is unique and that you cannot find it elsewhere.

You want people to visit your Instagram blog for the first time and be impressed with what they see.

First impressions on Instagram are everything.

People do not have sufficient attention when it comes to social media.

If your blog doesn't catch their eye or leave a first-time visitor with an impression, they will find it difficult to return to your blog.

When planning your content, you should always keep this in mind.

The pictures you upload from your everyday activities should be interesting.

Don't just upload a picture of you in the shop.

You can instead upload a picture of the items you brought from the store and use it as an opportunity to give advice on the best products to buy for different things, such as breakfast or cleaning.

The drop in your pictures should be attractive.

If you upload photos, make sure that the backgrounds are esthetic and appeal to your follower's visual senses, which is something you cannot afford to neglect.

The quotes and reflections that you share on your blog must be related to your audience.

This is not just one focus advice.

You will also know what kind of quotes and reflections to share when you understand your fan base.

If your Instagram blog is for teenagers and young adults, you should know that the titles you share relate to the typical millennial issues in their lives.

What is the importance of content quality?

Quality of content is something you cannot afford to neglect or disregard.

Again, your followers want to see visuals that will impress them—visuals that will talk to them and make them want to see more.

Don't sell yourself short with pictures you've just found online.

Followers won't take your posts seriously if they see that your posts are of bad quality.

If you upload pictures of your products, don't just post a picture of the product carelessly on any surface.

Arrange the product on an attractive surface and ensure that everything is consistent, esthetically or symmetrically pleasing.

If you upload quotes, let them be on a template that is designed and aesthetically pleasing.

If you don't know how to create your own templates from scratch, you can contact a designer who can do it for you, or you can search for an app that gives you templates.

Look for high-definition pictures when you use stock images for Instagram blogs.

Most inventory sites offer high-quality images, but you have to be careful.

When you see potential images that you would like to upload, view them in full size to make sure they are not grainy or pixelated.

High-quality content enhances the audience's visual experience.

Photographs that were taken carefully will also contribute to your blog's aesthetics.

When you run an Instagram blog, you have to pay attention to detail.

Mistakes That Should Be Avoided

Don't be overly promotional.

If your feed is filled with promotional content, your followers will receive more of a spam atmosphere from your blog.

If your followers feel that they are disconnected from your blog, they may stop working with your posts.

Some of your followers will eventually unfold. Make a balance between promoting your blog and engaging your followers actively.

Don't ignore the response/feedback you receive from your followers. **You should actively seek your followers' feedback.**

You can send them a questionnaire or talk to them to see what they really think about your blog.

The response you receive from them could help you to work in areas in which you do not perform well in and can work to capitalize on areas in which you do well in.

Do not neglect captions.

Try to prevent uploading images without subtitles.

Subtitles help your followers gain more insight into the uploaded image.

Captions are also what you use to communicate with your followers.

The right types of headings give your followers the context of your posts and they can also contribute to your audience's response.

Try not to go too far. Two-hundred characters should be sufficient enough to pass on a message.

Use emojis as well—they can catch the eye of the viewer.

Don't neglect your community.

Some people tend to think that their Instagram is just one way.

They ignore the comments and messages of their followers. This never plays well.

Your followers will feel that you are not interested in what they have to say, and they will flee.

They may not even pay attention to your blog at all. Never wait for your followers to reach you, perhaps try reaching out to them!

Try not to underutilize the application.

Use the Instagram stories, hashtags, and inboxes to communicate with your followers and colleagues.

Don't just take pictures.

Try attaching a link to your profile and explore the features. Instagram recently introduced a feature that allows you to upload multiple photos as a single post.

Try to make use of that.

The more features you use, the more content you create.

Chapter 10: Figuring Out Your Brand Voice

This is often the most nebulous part of figuring out any kind of social media, be it Instagram, Twitter, Facebook, Foursquare, or anything else out there. Your "brand voice" is the personality of your business. Just like individual people have personalities, so do individual brands.

For example, the brand voice of Chase Bank is going to be different than the brand voice of Urban Outfitters. Both of those businesses have different clientele that they are attempting to attract, as well as different expectations out of their prospective customers. People aren't expecting a bank's voice to be outright goofy, for example, and people aren't expecting Urban Outfitters to sound like they work for a bank.

The best way to figure out your brand voice is to think about your ideal customer. How old are they? Are they male or female? What kind of car do they drive? What sorts of clothing do they wear? How much money do they make? Do they have a family? What are their interests?

By building up the profile of your "perfect customer," you can then target more specifically what that perfect customer is looking for out of their favorite brands. While your Instagram account is representing your business, remember that people are not on social media for hard sells - they are on it for entertainment and engagement. So your brand voice needs to entertain and engage your perfect customer.

Just like your friends are attracted to you by virtue of your personality, your Instagram followers will be attracted to you by virtue of your brand voice.

Once you have figured out who your perfect customer is, you can try and reflect this into the creation of your brand voice.

A very popular exercise for people trying to create brand voices is to challenge yourself to describe your brand in three words.

Trustworthy? Fun? Serious? Playful? Offbeat? Traditional? Unique?

Once you have your three terms down, define them further. What exactly does "fun" mean in terms of your brand? Are you the kind of "fun" that involves practical jokes, or the kind of "fun" that involves clever word puns?

Once you have redefined your terms, then you have a brand chart with the sentiment that you are trying to express. For instance, a "fun" brand who has defined "practical jokes" as their kind of fun may get this across on Instagram by posting pictures of a whoopee cushion left mischievously on the seat of a coworker.

Figure out your ideal customer, figure out your brand voice, and then make concrete plans on how to get those sentiments across on your Instagram.

Chapter 11: Instagram Influencer Marketing

Facebook Ads, eBooks, YouTube Marketing, Twitter and Blogging, they are some of the new marketing methods that appear every day or every week and truly, they do help businesses boost their online confidence and marketing. But, it can be exciting to detect which trendy marketing strategies are real. We know there's one thing that reigns from all those methods: Influencer Marketing, truth! But what is the connection of Influencer Marketing to Instagram Marketing?

If you are not much familiar on what is Influencer Marketing, it is a form of marketing which focuses on utilizing key ambassadors to spread the concept and the message of your brand to their audiences, to your target market, and possibly to a larger market. Instagram has more than 800 million monthly users, and

70% of Instagram users have already searched for brands on the same platform who wanted to guzzle their content. That is why Instagram marketing is effective for your e-commerce business if used right.

Instead of marketing directly to a group of consumers, you may want to hire and inspire influencers to spread the word for you.

Well, Instagram has become a place for influencers, a lot of them had grown their audience from small to millions in a short period of time. These internet celebrities have enormous authority over a germinating audience of untouched consumers. They have agreat influence over their audience and it can impact to the latest trends available.

Are you working with one of them? So, you will be able to speed up the development of your product in a short period of time.

For your business or product, you should start identifying the right influencers to work with. This is somewhat the inflexible part of the whole process, you don't want to mess up things at this stage as it affects your whole marketing strategy. Take note, if influencers don't like working with your brand, then stop pleasing them, you don't have to pressure a relationship onto an influencer, if you kept on begging them, chances are they will praise your product in a fake way, ending in a lot of comments saying "spam" from the audience. Once you have found the perfect person for your project, offer to run a trial campaign before pursuing deeper on the relationship.

Using Instagram Analytics tools is important in order to track the important metrics such as comments, engagements, and call-to-action that has a great impact on your business.

It is to be noted that you should be involved with your team regarding the strategy for the campaign, in order to get updated on your campaigns. If you accomplish this efficiently, be amazed by the result and benefits that influencer marketing can have on your business. Instagram Influencers are users with a significant audience who can be one of your customers.

STOP BEING FRUSTRATED WITH INSTAGRAM MARKETING

You have finally decided to go for it and signed your business up for an Instagram account. Way to go! This is one of the most engaging social communities out there today. But what happens when you find yourself without enough time to spend on your account?

With Instagram, as with any other social media account, if you are not going to be an active participant, then you might as well not sign up.

This visual social network was not created with efficiency in mind, making it one of the most frustrating aspects of a brand's social media marketing strategyHere are some helpful tips on how to get the most out of the time you spend on the social network without sucking up all of your time.

1. Use a scheduling app

If you have been on social media long enough, then you know that there is a peak time for posting. It is different for each brand and depends largely on when your audience is the most active.

Do your research and find out when that peak time is for your followers. This makes it most likely to see engagement from your audience when you post. The ideal time to post on Instagram is not always going to be the most convenient for your schedule. For example, how can you make sure that you are posting those images at 5 p.m. every Friday when you have end-of-week meetings set up during that time?

Simple solution: employ a scheduling app. There are plenty of them out there. Find the one you like and line up the posts you want to add throughout the week or month. Schedule the date and time you want each post released. And then go on with your day.

2. Respond to comments with help

An important part of creating brand loyalty on social media is to take time to reply to your followers' comments. They want to know that their comments are being acknowledged.

This can be hard when your following grows and you start to get a lot of comments on your posts each day. Luckily, you can employ the help of apps to make it easy to reply back.

3. Cross-post with one app

Sometimes you want to share your Instagram post across all of the other networks that you are using. But how can you do that without having to spend a lot of time on your phone? Employ the If This, Then That app. IFTTT is a fantastic tool for helping brands cross-post their content without having to go in and manually post.

With this app, you create a sort of "recipe" that will save you time on social media. Basically, you create a formula of what you want to happen when you do something else.

With this app, you can choose to have the images you share on Instagram to automatically be shared on Twitter, for example. Today's technology, specifically the number of apps that are available, make it so easy to take control of your social media marketing and make it fit into your schedule. This is especially helpful when it comes to the time-consuming aspects of Instagram. What apps do you find the most helpful when it comes to social media marketing?

INSTAGRAM MARKETING, PROS AND CONS

If you are looking to bring in more clients, people turn to social media. But everything has Pros and cons...

Pros:

1. A picture is valuable: As is often said, a picture is worth a thousand words. Think about it, when running a company, one will want to use images to show off their product or service. This is especially important when selling food, weight loss products or any other items that people love to look at and enjoy. However, one can take it further and show off travel destinations or any number of things. Simply put, this is one of the best tips for using Instagram for business as a picture will really show visitors the true value of a product or service.

2. Viral: Without a doubt, when using the Internet to market a product, service or idea, one will want it to go viral. If a site or idea goes viral, you can make a lot of money and find plenty of new and excited visitors. For this reason, when using

Instagram, you need to make sure they provide true value to a visitor. Then, and only then, one can see the photo go viral, which will result in a lot of new visitors to the site.

They do the work for the company: When one shares a photo with their friends and so on, it can go viral. Not only that, when using Instagram, the followers will do most of the work. Provided a company offers an interesting photo, it will likely go viral. In the end, one should follow the best tips for using Instagram for business. That way, the followers will do the legwork.

Cons:

1. Younger crowd: Now, when looking to find new clients, you usually want to go after an older crowd. Yes, while a lot of teenagers and young adults use Instagram, not all of them have the cash to spend. However, there are chances to get them hooked and coming back when they are older. Either way, when looking for the best strategy for Instagram, one must remember that not all people can lay out any cash.

2. Not business-minded: When following their favorite celebrity online, a lot of people are not interested in anything but wasting idle time.

It means that a lot of people are simply looking to pass some time on the train and have no intention of spending any money.

Chapter 12: Engaging Micro Influencers To Rank Content

In order to get your content ranked using Micro Influencers, you should follow the steps below in order:

Post Content to your Feed - The first step is to get your "Shoppable Post" onto your Instagram Feed. You should include all of the Hashtags you want your content to rank on in the post description.

Send out an Email Blast - Next, you will want to copy the link to your Instagram post and email it to your entire list of Micro Influencers. The message should instruct them to "Like and Comment" on your post in order to win 20 bonus points. Set a time limit for the bonus points because you want as many Influencers engaging with your post as soon as possible.

Send out a Text Blast - You will want to make sure as many Influencers see your post as soon as possible by sending out a text message blast. While this can cost you a little bit of money, it's well worth the cost as Influencers who get a text message from you can easily open up the Instagram link on their phone and click a few buttons to like and comment on your post.

Once you follow these steps, your post should receive enough likes and comments in a short amount of time to get it ranked at the top of the Hashtag search results for the keywords you included in your post description.

As you can see, utilizing Micro Influencers is essential to getting your content ranked and visible to active consumers who are more likely to make a purchase from you. This is something "Macro Influencers" would never be able to accomplish on their own as Macro Influencers can't share your "Shoppable Instagram Posts" to their feeds.

STRATEGY TWO:

INCENTIVIZE INFLUENCER CREATED BRAND CONTENT

One of the best ways to grow your brand online is to get as much positive third-party content created by Influencers. This third-party endorsement of your products, services and brand are highly valuable. The posted content should also include an @YourUsername in the description to drive new followers directly to your Instagram account and a link to your website even though it won't be clickable.

Content produced by Influencers could consist of product review videos, product image posts with a shoutout and description of how much they love your product.

Running an Instagram Hashtag campaign will help you dominate the Hashtag search results with content about your brand and products on Hashtags that your customers are searching for. As Influencers create, post and share more content, your brands visibility will increase drastically in all the places it matters.

EXPECTED RESULTS

On average, an Influencer should create 10-30 pieces of content for your brand over a 3-month campaign period. If your campaign uses averages 1,000 engaged Influencers, that's 10k - 30k pieces of content about your brand being posted and discovered during your campaign. The great thing about this type of campaign is that this content is always up generating more branding opportunities and new followers long after your campaign is over.

TIP: You should provide a list of Hashtags Influencers should include in their content descriptions.

STRATEGY THREE:

CREATE AND PROMOTE A UNIQUE HASHTAG

Creating a unique Hashtag specific to your brand will allow you to keep track of Influencers who post content about your brand when they include your unique hashtag in the description. Running a "Hashtag" photo contest will help you incentivize Influencers to create and share more brand focused content. When creating your unique Hashtag, make sure it's not already being used.

Next, pick a word that is targeted to your niche, for instance, if you have a Yoga Apparel Brand, you might want to include the word "Yoga" in your hashtag string along with a unique twist like #YogaMammaApparel. This will allow your hashtag to pop up in the suggested hashtags that pull up in the search results when someone starts typing in a similar word like "#YogaPants".

This will drive more discoverability to your unique Hashtag. As more Influencers create and post content with your Hashtag in it, it will start to trend and become more visible.

InstaTout offers advanced Hashtag promotion contests that manage every aspect of these types of campaigns.

Chapter 13: Tips And Tricks For Creating More Effective Videos

Every business wants to make an impression on Instagram. Every business wants to leave its mark among the millions of Instagrammers out there on the platform in the hopes of making more sales. With more than 20 billion pictures and videos on its platform, Instagram is becoming an indispensable tool that marketers cannot live without. To be that one brand that stands out among the 20 billion contents, you need to create mind-blowing content that is going to make your audiences sit up and take notice. You need mind-blowing videos.

In the chapter, you'll be walking through some of the best tips and tricks available to help you create some truly staggering video content that will put your business on the map. Instagram has made some big changes to its platform since it first got started, and a lot of these changes have been extremely beneficial for brands with a business account. New tools and advanced features have brought with it a whole new realm of possibilities for marketers. Once you know just how to take full advantage of these tools, Instagram for advertising is going to be your new best friend.

Getting to Know the Instagram Culture

Business and brands have gone international. Worldwide shipping is now everywhere and offered by just about every business, broadening their customer reach like never before. However, there is one mistake that a lot of marketers still tend to make when it comes to advertising their products and services - ignoring the cultures of the specific regions which they're targeting. Your audience based in the United States is going to be different from the ones based in Europe or Asia. They would have different expectations and perceptions. What works for one region might not work well in another.

Let's observe a campaign which was conducted by Pepsi for example. Pepsi came up with the slogan **Pepsi Brings You Back to Life**, but what they didn't take note of was that when translated, it became **Pepsi Brings Your Ancestors Back from the Grave.** This may not seem like such a big deal, but it was an extremely huge mistake and counter-productive to the company's efforts to bring the brand global. Even before you map out your video content, you should conduct thorough research into all your target markets and observe the differences in culture. It would be great if you could get in touch with a local native to help you out with the process.

How and Why Instagram Is Different

Instagram is a social media platform unlike any other. True, other social media platforms do have video and image sharing content too, but none of them can do it quite as well as Instagram can. No social media platform has been able to match Instagram just yet in terms of image and video quality and expectations. Another common mistake made by a lot of marketers is assuming that each social media platform is interchangeable. What works well for one is going to work just as well for the other, especially if you're sharing the same content from the same ad campaign. Not entirely true, because each social media platform has its own algorithm which drives your viewership, and it doesn't meet the requirements, your content is not going to get put in front of your target audiences the way that you hope it would be.

Instagram is a platform where a brand gets to show their personality. Here's the thing about Instagram's video content though - you only have a couple of seconds to get your point across. That old saying "time is of the essence" is very apt indeed when it comes to Instagram's video advertising because with only seconds to tell your story, you're going to have to make every second count. Another catch is that while you need to focus on telling your brand's story in a matter of seconds, you need to do it in a way that doesn't seem too much like an ad, or **too commercial**. Your brands shouldn't give the appearance of being too corporate when it comes to content, because that's how audiences are turned off. Starbucks is one example of a brand who has mastered this side of Instagram.

The company has curated their content and their brand's story so well that they have successfully marketed themselves as a brand who is your artsy and fun BFF. And they have done it so well that they've successfully avoided appearing too commercial-heavy. Yet, almost every photo and video that you're going to find on the company's social media profile is very distinctly branded in one way or another. It could be a simple shot of just a green straw that is sticking out of a whipped cream mountain, or it could be a picture or a video of a paper cup which a fan has elaborately and artistically decorated. By incorporating a lot of user-generated content and fan-made images, the company has successfully reframed their content to help build a sense of community that the audience can relate too. They have combined successful branding, aesthetic variation in content and avoided the "hard-sell" aspect because their content does not blatantly make it obvious that it is in fact, an advertisement at the end of the day.

Successfully marketing video content on Instagram is going to require some emulation of what Starbucks has done. Diving into the insights of the social media platform is going to help you out here because you need to have all the available information possible on your customers **before** you can create a content which resonates with them. Observe them, find them, follow them, engage with them, reach out to them, connect with them, do whatever it takes to build that relationship which is going to allow you to dig deeper into what is going to work for your audience. Likewise, you have to make it easy for your audience to **connect to your brand** on the social media platform. Ensure that the bio section of your profile is filled with all the important details, provide a clear link and make your profile public so the content is easily viewable by everyone.

The main purpose of having an Instagram profile for your business is so that you will be able to share your brand's image and video content, while simultaneously building credibility.

Videos Worthy of Attention

For your brand to be the one that is worth watching, you need to create video content which is worth watching. Take this as a unique opportunity to become a great storyteller, to showcase your brand in a whole new light. It's not about trying to rebrand your image, but rather, it is about showing just how versatile and creative your brand can be. Quality content is the hook that will keep your audiences coming back for more.

The challenge for a lot of brands is creating great video content frequently. Content which is good enough to drive sales conversions. As a brand, you **must** give people a reason to **want** to follow you. Your video content needs to be inspiring enough that your audience is not going to just swipe through it and move onto the next content. Brands need to have the right content strategy and be headed in the right direction for their Instagram video ads to successfully make an impact. How do you begin creating video content that your Instagram audience is going to love? By following some of the tips below:

Blending In Organically: Your video content needs to be able to blend in organically into the news feed of your audience. Take a leaf out of Starbucks's books and start creating content which does not blatantly stand out as a commercial. You're competing against millions of other brands on Instagram for the attention of your audience, and if you don't want your audience to scroll past you on their news feed faster than the speed of light, you need to blend in so well that it takes them several seconds to realize that this is an ad content which they are looking at. Blend in, be natural and be one with your audience's news feed. Those are the pointers that you need to keep in mind when creating your video content.

One Theme, One Topic: A video content with far too much going on is only going to overwhelm your audience. Even though you only have a couple of seconds to get your point across, this does not mean that you should jam pack your video with every single detail to a point that it's going to confuse and possibly even frustrate your audience because they'll have a hard time keeping up or absorbing the information. Doing that is only going to make them scroll past your video content even more (remember that fitting in organically is critical to capturing attention). Instead, when setting out to create your videos, decide on a single theme or a single topic at any given time. There is no necessity to cram all the information in at once because you'll have plenty of opportunities to create videos on a frequent basis which can highlight different key points or aspects of your business. In fact, the more spread out your information, the better because it's just going to give you more material to work with. This way, you avoid being stuck for ideas about what to post.

Being Wise with Your Captions: If you didn't already know this, Instagram does not play audio automatically. The audience needs to tap on the video for the sound, and that is a problem for many marketers.

Relying too much on just audio alone to convey announcements and messages runs the risk of your messages being lost in translation. If it takes a while for your audience to realize that they need to tap on the video for the sound to come through, they're going to miss the first half of what your video ad was about. Especially if there are no captions accompanying the video content. Captions are a must for your Instagram video ads, but use it sparingly and use it wisely. Your audience does not want to see a bunch of texts and several long sentences zooming across their screen. Short, succinct words and sentences are your best bet to work with. Squarespace has successfully mastered the technique of capturing their audience's attention without the need for any sound accompaniment by simply using two words in their ad content - "Squarespace Presents". Simple, concise, to the point, effective.

Videos That Solve a Problem: Video content which helps users solve a problem is one that gets them all excited. Which means they'll be a lot more likely to stick around and engage with your videos because it is giving them something of value, something that they need and want. By helping them identify and solve a problem, you're in effect creating a bond with them and forging a connection. Problem-solving videos show the audience that the brand understands and more importantly, cares about what they're going through. Plus, it makes your content more organic when you're not constantly focused on just selling, selling, selling all the time. Audiences will get bored after a while of the constant hard-sell and will turn away from your content when they've had enough of it.

Chapter 14: How To Sell On Your Page

Selling on Instagram takes place over three simple steps: creating sales funnels, marketing to the people who are most likely to pay you, and using display ads to reach those people effectively. In this chapter, we are going to explore these three selling opportunities and how you can leverage them to maximize your conversions through the Instagram platform. While there are many ways to word your sales copy and many areas to post to on Instagram, there are generally three ways that will allow you to find followers who want to pay for your products. Sales funnels are the first one, and they are used to drive people around your profile in a systematic way that ultimately results in them clicking on your link and purchasing products. These are the easiest ones to create, but they do take some practice, as it can be challenging to know how to smoothly drive people around your profile through your stories, posts, and IGTV videos. The second way that you can sell on Instagram is by drawing people into your actual storefront if you have one through local marketing.

The rest of this book has been dedicated to locating global clients, so we are going to put emphasis solely on attracting local clients if you are running a brick and mortar business in your city. Finally, displaying ads is another great way to sell since ads make it clear that there is something for sale in the first place. You can use display ads as either posts or stories, depending on what your budget is and where you feel you are going to get the most traction from your ads.

Creating Sales Funnels on Instagram

Since Instagram offers plenty of opportunities to connect with your followers, it is easy for you to build

Instagram into your sales funnel and start creating a higher conversion ratio through your account. Making your Instagram sales funnel will take some planning because you need to ensure that every channel on the platform is driving people through a "funnel" until they ultimately land on your website and find your products so that they can begin shopping with you. There are two different ways where you can drive people into your website: directly or indirectly. Directly driving people to your site means that you make one post, and it immediately sends people through to your website so that they can start shopping with your brand.

You do this anytime you make a post that encourages people to go to the link in your bio. Start shopping for the product or service that you were talking about in your post. You can also have the same impact by sending people to your link through your stories or your IGTV channel. As long as you are directly asking someone to go to your link, you are directly channeling them through your funnel. This means that indirect conduits will have a direct element since, at some point, you are going to need to bounce people from your Instagram profile to your website. Indirect sales funnels are a great way to provide your audience with plenty of information before they leave your page to check out your site as you have directed them to. Since you are driving them through two or three posts, you can provide plenty of diverse insight and information on your product, service, or brand before they ultimately land on your website. There are many different ways that you can drive people around your Instagram profile, depending on what it is that you are trying to accomplish and what type of content you have to offer. For example, you can encourage someone watching your story to go check out your post, and then, when they check out the post, you can have a piece written that helps them to check out your latest IGTV video, and then that video can lead people to your website. You can also have one post that directs people to your site and then use your stories, IGTV, and live video feed to drive everyone over to that story first, where they read your content before then clicking over to your website.

How you choose to funnel people through your page and to your website is up to you, though you should always be doing this or working toward building a funnel to ensure that you are directing people over to where they can pay for your products or services. That being said, refrain from making every single post, story, and video according to your marketing needs or funneling people around because people will quickly catch what you are doing, and they will stop following you. Some of your posts should be solely based on attracting new audience members to your profile through valuable content, interesting information, high-quality images, and relationship-building strategies like those outlined previously in this book. Of course, if you are building a sales funnel on your Instagram profile, it is only natural that you include that sales funnel on your website, too. When people land on your website, they should be very clearly drawn through your site to learn more about who you are and what you have to offer before landing on a page where they can look at your products or services. This way, they already know that they like your brand, and they want to shop with you before they even land on your sales page.

You should also have an e-mail capture popup appear on your website so that you can start capturing people's emails and building an email newsletter into your funnel. Remember that some people will need to land on your website several times before they pay for your products or services. You are going to need to continually funnel people over to your website and make your offers known so that people can continually land on your website and then make the decision to go ahead and purchase from you. Believe it or not, the more people land on your site, the more connected they feel to you, so even if they do not buy right away, they will remember their previous visits to your website and will begin to feel encouraged to shop with you the more they visit.

Local Marketing Strategies

Most of the strategies that we have been using to achieve new prospect clients are relatively broad and work great if you are running a global or remote business where the location of your clients is not entirely necessary. However, if you are running a local business, you are going to want to approach your marketing slightly differently so that you can reach your target audience in your local area. The way that you target your local market is simple, though it will require some intention and practice on your behalf to make sure that you are reaching the people that you are meant to achieve. The first thing that you should be doing is looking up local hashtags, especially ones that are explicitly related to your industry. For example, if you are a candle maker, you can use hashtags like "#newyorkcandles" or "#calgarycandles," which are unique to your local area. You can also start using hashtags that are specific to entrepreneurs or certain relevant hobbies in your local area. So when you take pictures, you can use these hashtags and connect with other people in your area who would also be interested in what you have to offer.

By using local hashtags in this way, you can ensure that you are reaching people who are close to you and accessing the local market, which will likely be more relevant to your target audience. Another way that you can market to your local audience is in person using strategies to get the people you meet in person on your Instagram account since you are likely using other in-person outreach methods to connect with your local audience. You can use this as an opportunity to have people follow you on Instagram.

They are then using Instagram to keep them up-to-date on your latest offers, sales, and new products or services. Many brands will do this by informing people about their Instagram by word of mouth, including their Instagram handle on their business cards, and by putting their Instagram handle somewhere in their physical shop so that people can find it and see it. A particularly unique way that people are marketing in-person is by offering a photo op in their store where people can take pictures. In the photo op, they will generally include their store name and a unique hashtag that people can use to tag the store and their unique hashtag in their photograph, which not only connects the local audience with the brand but also creates free marketing.

Another similar practice that has been used in coffee shops and cafés is having the Instagram logo drawn on the coffee board with the company's handle written next to it and a live tracker of how many followers the company has. Every time someone new follows them, they increase the number on the board so that they can share their growth with their audience right there in the store. Ideally, you should be using as many different strategies as you can to drive your online audience to your in-person store, and your in-person store to your online platforms. The more you can connect with people both online and offline, the more relevant you stay in their lives, and therefore, the more likely you are to gain sales through your Instagram marketing strategies.

Designing Display Ads

Another way that you can drive up sales from Instagram is by using display ads, which can be featured either in newsfeeds or story feeds, depending on what type of ad you choose to pay for. You can use one or the other, or ideally, you can use both on your platform so that you are reaching as many people as you can, based on their preferred method of consuming content on Instagram. Should you have followers that prefer to consume content both through their feeds and their stories, they will come across your ads twice as often, which means that they will be twice as likely to click through and see what you have to offer. There are three different types of display ads that you can provide on Instagram: videos, static images, and carousel images. Carousel images will not work on Instagram story ads, so you will need to choose a different method of advertising if you are going to be advertising through Instagram stories. Each ad has its unique benefits, though the theme is that the more you get your brand in front of your audience, the more likely they are to click through and check out your website or follow you.

Additionally, your display ads will target more than just your existing audience, which means that you have an additional channel working for you to help you bring in new followers and customers through Instagram. You can set up your Instagram advertisements by going to your Facebook account and opening up an ads management account. Then, you can go ahead and tap "Create Ad" on the left side of the screen and follow the prompts provided to you. Facebook's ads manager will ask you what your goals are with your advertisement, what you want the people who see your ad to do, and how you want to design the ad. You can then create it and choose which platforms you want it to run on, how, for how long, and with what budget. You will also determine who you want to see the ad based on their demographics, interests, and whether or not they are already following you. Once you have set in these parameters, all you have to do is publish the ad, and it will begin showing up on all the areas where you said it would.

When it comes to displaying advertisements, you must use high-quality images. This is very important for what you are advertising so that your audience immediately knows what you are sharing with them. You also need to use a caption that is direct, engaging, and interesting. Make sure that you give these posts your all so that you are creating something worthy of people stopping and paying attention to what it is that you are advertising for them. If you are not tech-savvy, or you find yourself struggling to make compelling images for advertisements, you might consider hiring a professional social media advertising agency to support you in creating high-quality publications. Many individuals are in the business of creating posters and putting them to work on social media so that you can start seeing better results from your paid ads. While this will cost you more money since you are paying someone else to design your ads, they will also be more likely to gain traction, making them worth your investment.

Chapter 15: Instagram Hacks For Taking Really Good Photos

If you couldn't get this until now, Instagram is a great place to market your business. The photo sharing platform has all the right tools for promoting your brand. However, since the majority of the posts on this platform are photos, how can you stand out among the tough competition out there?

The answer to this is by using good photos for your posts. Making your photos attractive and of the best quality gives you the edge you need to help boost your page.

It is true that your photos must be top-notch but the question is how can you take great photos that will be of the best quality?

Here are some tips that will help you take the best photos:

1. Plan ahead

Planning ahead before taking the picture is a good way to start the process of taking good photos. You are advised to think about your brand and what you really want to offer your audience. Advanced planning gives you a good idea about what you want to do. That will give you a blueprint to work with.

2. Don't be obsessed with people's thoughts

When you are through with your plan, take the time to find you what you really like. Your thoughts shouldn't be focused primarily on what the Instagram community wants from you, or the type of photo is the most popular amongst the members of the community. If you give heed to these thoughts, you will defeat your goal of getting the best picture before you even took out the camera.

3. Use natural sources of light

One of the most important factors you must consider is lighting. It is the key to the overall beauty of your photos. Note that even the best photo-editing app with the most complex filter can never make a good job of a poorly-lit photo. Using natural sources of light will give your photos the right illumination. If you must take any photo outdoors, you should consider doing so early in the morning, late in the afternoon, or overcast days. These periods are when you can get the best shots.

4. Use your eyes before your camera

Your eyes still remain an important and efficient tool for taking good photos. It is customary to see people taking a couple of pictures, comparing them, and then making their choice. Instead of towing that path and wasting time taking tens of shots before settling for the best, use your eyes before using the camera.

This requires that you look at the object critically, frame the picture with your eyes, and observe the object for some time. This may give you a new perspective for looking at the object so that you can get the best shot after taking a few pictures.

5. Use the grid feature

It is good to bring your composition in when attempting to take a picture. Whenever you want to take a picture, you can make the best job of it by turning on the grid. You can watch the elements overlapping through your viewfinder or on the screen until you get the perfect conditions for shooting. That will enhance the beauty of your photo.

6. Use the point of interest

A common feature of all good photos is the presence of a point of interest. It may be someone in the foreground or a great landscape with sharp lines that focuses the viewer's eyes. Great photos are known for having more than one point of interest without them overlapping and creating a sense of clutter. Try to let your photo reveal a little information about the place or person. Let it tell a story about the point of interest.

7. Watch out for moments

Another way to make your photo great is by letting your pictures have great moments. Let the moments be about the subjects or subject you want to shoot. Look for some natural moments such as extreme, peak, settled, or emotional moments. Either of these moments will make the picture interesting.

If there are unwanted pieces of information, stay away from them. The unwanted information may detract from the great moment and impact the picture negatively. You can only be pardoned if the unwanted information contributes to the overall beauty of the image.

Your goal is to have a clean image, free of unwanted clutter, that draws the attention of the viewers directly to the story you want to tell.

8. Strong shapes, colors, and lines are good

One of the qualities of a good Instagram image is strong colors and well-defined lines. The photo should contain some elements that will loom large in your camera's frame so that it can easily draw the attention of the viewers. Through personal training and regular practice, you will develop the skills for conveying some emotions with your pictures.

9. Use third-party apps

There are tons of third-party apps that you can use to make your pictures stand out. These apps come in different forms and for a wide variety of functions. You can explore the functionalities of these apps to add to the overall beauty of your images.

An app that is good for simulating a slow shutter to some moving objects, such as blurry water, can create a long-exposure effect. The effect will be more pronounced on waterfalls or incredibly large bodies of water. That will give you the perfect condition to show high contrast between the sharp, still surroundings and the water.

10. Use light from strange sources

If you compare your phone camera with traditional cameras, you will see a clear distinction. The lens of the phone camera has a different way of absorbing light than the camera. That makes it possible for the phone camera to see light from some strange places such as behind the object or above it.

If you move the object around without taking your eyes off it through your phone camera, you will see the object as it transforms until you can see the rays of light on your lens. The light will have a powerful impact on the image. This is the moment you are waiting for. Take your shot right here.

11. Leverage the burst mode

When taking a picture, you may see the need to make a moment stand still without losing its detail. If you want to do that, shoot in daylight or in a well-lit space so that you can use a fast shutter speed.

Ensure that you tap the screen to make it possible to lock focus on the object manually. You can also make the exposure perfect by using the slide bar before taking the shot. With burst mode, you have a perfect tool that will be useful when choosing the most appropriate moment for the picture.

12. Shoot from a wide variety of angles

You can try to take your pictures from viewpoints that look quite unusual. If you consider a view to be normal, it can actually look awesome if you shoot it from a different perspective than through the perspective you see.

Consider shooting from as many angles as possible to make your pictures more appealing. You can try the right-down or up-high position and see the impact it has on your image.

13. Use props

You should consider using different objects, and observe their impact on the story you are trying to tell. By taking your environment and the background of the object into consideration, you can do a good job of making your photo look great by making the scene come alive.

14. Use a bad weather to your advantage

While some people curl up at the idea of having to deal with bad weather while shooting, you can use the bad weather to your advantage. Whenever there is fog, snow, or rain you should go out there and find a way to make the best use of that weather to shoot a unique picture. An experienced photographer once suggested that you should use bad weather to make good photographs.

15. Use the puddles after the rain

After a rainfall, go out there and take awesome photos. The puddles will give you reflections that you can utilize to contribute beauty to your pictures. That background will be great for taking interesting pictures and you shouldn't hesitate to use them.

16. Consider using white space

White space is fun to use. They add uniqueness and beauty to your picture. Take a look at some masterpieces like the latest catalog of J.Crew, or an outstandingly beautiful home. What common feature do they have? Both of these use tons of white space.

You can imitate them and bring such an impression to your picture so that you can make your Instagram feed neat and clutter free. How you feel about those pictures when you see them mirrors the way others will feel when viewing your Instagram feed when it has enough white space.

The best way to have a good shot with white space is to look for white backgrounds when shooting. If you want to photograph a person, you can shoot in front of a white wall to have that effect on your picture.

If you want to shoot an object, a white window sill or a piece of foam board should be used for photographing the object in order to add the white space effect.

Some font apps also have such feature. You can try WordSwag and use it to put an impressive quote on your photo to give it that white space effect. That will give your feed some breathing room.

17. Take advantage of the portrait mode

Instagram has a new portrait mode that you can take advantage of. You can use it to lay emphasis on the length of a particular scene. You can also use it to tell a detailed story that just isn't possible with a square crop.

18. Add more elements

Adding more elements to your scale will make your photo look great. Adding scale to your image can be done by simply including a person in the image's frame. You can try different poses within the same scene to find the best one that will add to the beauty of your image.

19. Layers are handy

Using layers for your images makes it possible to convey a perfect message to the viewer. The goal is to let the viewers share the same point of view with you. Using these will give your audience a good view of your brand because they see your brand exactly the way you want them to see it.

20. Use patches of light

You can find patches of light in different places. The street lamp and the rays of sunlight are perfect sources for these patches of light. During a photography session, find them and use them to enhance your skills.

An important attribute of using patches of light emanating from the sun is that the patches will always give you a variety of backgrounds to use. Make use of that to give your audience a perfect picture.

21. Use the dusk to your advantage

Even when the sun is going down you can still stay out to take beautiful pictures. Although we have limited vision when the sun goes down, modern cameras have better ability to pick up light than humans.

This is a good way to give your audience something beautiful. By leveraging the unusual power of the camera to capture the captivating moments of a sunset, you can give your audience something truly amazing.

22. Move as physically possible to your subject

You can get more than you bargain for if you can move closer to your object as much as possible. Whether you want to shoot animals or people, it is advisable that you get close to them. That creates the right emotion and intimacy in your work. Your audience will appreciate the output and the sense of intimacy associated with the picture. Move closer to the object and use the widest focal length you can. That will bring the object into perspective, and will fill the frame of the photo. The result is a subject that is popped out so much that this cannot be achieved without the lens.

If you are an iPhone user, Moment has a good wide angle lens that will give you the best results. On the other hand, DSLR users may find the 16-35 mm lens very useful.

23. Use your phone's accessories

When considering taking a good shot, a lens attachment can make all the difference in improving your photo. If you want to add some character to the photo, consider using a wide angle lens.

24. Your edits should be simple

The availability of different editing tools has turned some people into editing freaks. While some people keep their edits simple, some have a tendency over edit their shots. Experience has shown that over-edited photos can lose its appeal. Therefore, when using filters to give your photos the best look, resist the urge to overdo it.

Whichever editing tool you use, be moderate. Don't push a photo too far from its real natural state. Users won't find it attractive that way. However, subtle tweaks are cool and will help the image to maintain its natural look.

A study by the social media scientist at HubSpot, Dan Zarella, revealed that photos that don't have too much color saturation in them get more likes than the others that are over-edited. What else did the stats say? Such images can get almost 600% likes more than other posts.

25. Always aim for quality

You can up your game on Instagram by curating your feed and making sharing a better part of your activities as opposed to posting. The implication here is that you should be selective about lighting and composition. That will give you tons of high-quality images to choose from to share with your audience.

26. Make practice a way of life

You can't get it right at your first attempt. You need tons of hours of regular practice sessions to master the art of taking beautiful pictures. If you have the time to make regular practices, you will gradually know your tools and the best ways to take amazing shots.

Always be ready to get a good shot whenever an interesting scene, location, moment, or light pops up. Cultivate the habit of doing a good job composing good photos. You can also take a couple of frames of the same object to get the best results while you also pay close attention to the editing.

The results will be sharp, clean photos that will wow you with natural colors and appealing tones.

The hours of practice sessions will be fully rewarding as the appreciation for your posts increase, and as more followers join your base.

Conclusion

Thanks for making it through to the end of this book. Let's hope it was informative and able to provide you with all of the tools you need to achieve your goals whatever they may be.

Instagram's strength lies in its ability to reach people from across the globe the way conventional methods of advertising can never do. With various tools and features which are optimized for advertising, brands are able to market themselves in a completely new and creative way. Not only can businesses interact with customers from all over the world, but they can now do so 24/7 if they want to simply by just logging into the social media site. Advertising is a crucial element to a business's online success, and now that you know how to avoid the common mistakes which are usually made, you'll be able to create more effective advertising campaigns from here on out.

The best tip to keep in mind with your advertising efforts is that you want your brand to always remain visible to your audience. Your brand and your Instagram profile should always be easily accessible at any time, anywhere. Creating awesome content that keeps your customers and audiences coming back for more, and if you can avoid the common mistakes that a lot of marketers tend to make, it is entirely possible to create advertising campaigns which a going to make a big difference to your business. The best advice you can follow is to find what works for your business.